Robert Bruce

KING OF SCOTS

By the same author

ANTIQUES OF THE FUTURE

AIRMAILS 1870–1970

COMMEMORATIVE MEDALS

GREEK AND ROMAN COINS

AN INTRODUCTION TO SMALL ANTIQUES

COMMEMORATIVE POTTERY AND PORCELAIN

THE ANIMALIERS

GLASS PAPERWEIGHTS

Robert Bruce

KING OF SCOTS

JAMES A. MACKAY

LONDON
ROBERT HALE & COMPANY

First published in Great Britain 1974

ISBN 0 7091 4718 X

Robert Hale & Company
63 Old Brompton Road
London S.W.7

PRINTED IN GREAT BRITAIN BY
BRISTOL TYPESETTING CO. LTD
BARTON MANOR - ST. PHILIPS
BRISTOL

Contents

For

Colin Greaves

Illustrations

CREDITS

The above illustrations numbered 2, 3, 4, 6, 7, 8, 9, 10, 11 and 13 are reproduced by courtesy of the Scottish Tourist Board; number 14 is reproduced by courtesy of the National Galleries of Scotland; number 18 is Crown Copyright and reproduced by permission of the Department of the Environment.

Maps and Charts

Scotland and Northern England

CHAPTER I

The Bruces of Annadale

THE BRUCES, like many of the other noble families of the Middle Ages, could trace their ancestry with certainty back to the rabble of adventurers who flocked to the banner of William of Normandy in 1066. Less certainly, but with a degree of probability, the Bruces claimed a lineage which extended back at least another hundred years, to the Vikings of the far north. Traditionally they were descended from Lödver, the Norse Earl of Orkney who flourished in the tenth century. His son, the Earl Sigurt, fell at the battle of Clontarf in 1014, when the Irish under Brian Boru routed the Vikings and broke their hold over eastern Ireland. Sigurt's second wife Olith (Alice) was a granddaughter of Malcolm II, King of Scots, and from this marriage sprang Torphin, progenitor of the Earls of Caithness. By an unnamed first wife, however, Sigurt produced four sons, Somerled, Brusee, Eynor and Whelp. Brusee's son Rognvald (1012–46) became Earl of Gothland in 1033 and married Ostrida, daughter of Rognvald Walfsen. They had two sons and four daughters whose marriages and subsequent careers illustrate the cosmopolitanism of the Vikings in the early eleventh century. Ingreda married Turbrand, ancestor of the Norman family of De la Val, Margrita married Thorbrand of Denmark, Hamilliana wed Ottalo of Russia and Arlogia married Thurstan be Beck who came to England with the Conqueror in 1066.

The two sons Eyliff and Ulf migrated to Normandy and embraced Christianity in 1034, changing their names to Regenvald and Robert respectively. Regenvald married Felicia de Hastings and fathered William de Brus, Lord of Brember in

Sussex and ancestor of the Norman family of de Braose. The younger brother Robert married Emma of Brittany and died in 1066 at Brix, a few kilometres south of Cherbourg in the Cotentin peninsula. The elder son, Alan, became lord of Brix and married Agnes, daughter of Simon de Montford. He came to England as a page to Emma of Normandy (the consort successively of Ethelred the Unready and his vanquisher, Cnut of Denmark). Emma's great nephew was William the Conqueror and both Alan of Brix and his younger brother Adelme (or Adam) were staunch supporters of his claim to the English throne.

Adam de Brix (or Brus, as it is sometimes rendered) subsequently served the Conqueror well by ravaging Yorkshire and reducing Anglo-Saxon resistance to Norman rule by terrorizing the native inhabitants. As a reward for his services he was given 34 manors in the north of England and the lordship of Skelton. He took as his wife Emma, daughter of Sir William Ramsay, and died in 1094. His eldest son was Robert de Brus, Lord of Cleveland, while the second son, William, became the first Prior of Guisborough. His daughter, Rossilina, married Walter de Morville (whose ancestral home was close to Brix in Brittany) and who later became Great Constable of Scotland.

Robert de Brus, the first of this name, married Agnes, daughter of Fulke de Paganell, and had a long and successful career as one of the great magnates of northern England. He served King Henry I as a justice, or royal "overseer", and took a distinguished—if somewhat ironic—part in the Battle of the Standard in 1138 when a Scottish invasion, led by David I, was repulsed. Scotland had only just become a united kingdom, unified in the person of King David who had joined the ancient realm of the Picts and Scots to Strathclyde and the Lothians, and he had sought to consolidate his position at the expense of his southern neighbour, then entering the long, weary years of anarchy and civil war between the supporters of Stephen and Matilda. As a young man David had been captured by the Anglo-Normans and brought up at the court of Henry I who created him Earl of Huntingdon in 1114. Robert de Brus held land of the Honour of Huntingdon, with manors in Rutland, while his brother-in-law, Walter de Morville, held land from Earl David in Northamptonshire.

It is not surprising, therefore, that David should turn to these Norman noblemen whenever he needed help in quelling the unruly elements among the native Scots. In 1130, for example, Angus and Malcolm of Moray, great-grandsons of Macbeth, attempted to displace David who appealed to the Norman barons of northern England for help. They rallied so effectively to his side that the revolt was easily quelled. David rewarded these Norman warriors with grants of land in strategic areas in order to contain pockets of unrest. Great military fiefs were established in Moray and the north-east, and also around the Celtic fringe area of Galloway in the south-west. But this policy was initiated about the time when, in 1124, David succeeded his brother Alexander as King of Scotland. In or about that year he granted Annandale to the Lord of Cleveland with the object of creating a buffer against the wild and lawless Gallovidians.

The river Annan, from which this district takes its name, has its source in the Devil's Beef Tub, a spectacular gully on the northern boundary of modern Dumfriesshire. Other streams join it near the modern town of Moffat and thence it meanders through a broad-bottomed plain, heading almost due south to enter the Solway Firth opposite Bowness. Towards the south the valley widens, but is bounded by hills constituting some of the wildest countryside in southern Scotland and the refuge, generations later, of the Covenanters. On its southwestern side Annandale is bounded by the great swamp known as Lochar Moss—now partially drained but, until comparatively recent times, virtually impassable. To the east of the Lochar Moss a line of hills traverses the plain and on the Annandale side of these hills nestles the royal burgh of Lochmaben, ringed about by a necklace of small lochs. At the mouth of the river Annan stands the town of the same name. In the twelfth century Lochmaben and Annan were the twin headquarters of the Bruces and the surrounding countryside was governed from their respective castles. Both fortresses possessed great strategic importance, protecting the natural route from the west of Scotland to Carlisle and northern England; today, the motorway which now links London and Glasgow runs barely three miles to the east of these towns. The Bruces of Annandale were, in fact if not in name, the Wardens of the Western Marches, protecting the trade route and the gateway to Scotland—as much from the wild men of Galloway as from the English.

The first Robert to hold land in Annandale was already well on in years when he received the grant from King David, and when the question arose as to where his loyalty lay he had no qualms about assigning his lands and rights in Scotland to his younger son. This dilemma was occasioned in 1138 when David chose to invade England—nominally in support of the Empress Maud or Matilda against the usurper Stephen of Blois, but in reality in his own interest. Shortly before this ill-starred campaign commenced Brus divested himself of the lordship of Annandale in favour of his son Robert, known as *le meschin* (the younger). The elder Brus fought valiantly under Archbishop Thurstan of York and the sacred Standard of St. Peter at Cowton Moor and was instrumental in securing victory to the English side. His son Robert took his place among the great barons of Scotland on the opposing side. There is a touching story about the old man and his son meeting on the eve of battle but neither was able to persuade the other to refrain from taking part.

Robert le Meschin was fourteen years old at the time of the Battle of the Standard and is represented traditionally as an impetuous youngster. While his elder brother succeeded to the Bruce lands in Yorkshire and was the ancestor of Earls of Chester and the Percys of Northumberland, Robert consolidated the family position in Scotland without necessarily severing his English connections. He lived to a ripe old age and died in 1196, but his career was dogged by domestic misfortune apparently brought about by a curse placed upon his family by St. Malachy.

St. Malachy was a famous Irish ecclesiastic who reformed the tribal churches in Ireland and brought them into line with the doctrines and practices of the Continent. He became Archbishop of Armagh and, during the last ten years of his life, was Papal Legate in Ireland. In 1148 he set out on a pilgrimage to Rome but turned aside with ill health at Clairvaux where he died, in the arms of St. Bernard, on 2nd November of that year. The Lanercost Chronicle, written two centuries later, recounts how

> The bishop reached Annan, the capital of the dale, where he sought refreshment from the lord of the place. This must

have been Robert de Brus, lord of Annandale, the son of the original grantee. Made warmly welcome, and seated at an ornate table on the north side of the Brus's hall, he was partaking of food along with two fellow clerics, his companions, when he heard the servants discussing the fate of a robber who was about to undergo sentence. Shortly after, the Brus himself entered with hearty greetings to his guests. The bishop's heart, however, was filled with the thought of the poor wretch without, whose doom was so near. He at once appealed to the Brus who as baron, with jurisdiction of pit and gallows, held the thief's fate in the hollow of his hand. "I demand," said the humane and warm-hearted Irishman, "as a pilgrim that, since judgment of blood has never yet violated the place of my presence, if the man has committed any crime, you will grant me his life." The bishop's noble host nodded not in courtesy but in deceit; and acting according to the prudence of this world which is folly with God, he secretly gave orders to hang the thief. Meanwhile the bishop, in happy ignorance, rejoicing that he had saved a human life, finished his repast and prepared to go on his way. Before starting he bestowed his blessing on the Brus's house and table and household. As he was departing, imagine his surprise to behold hanging on the gallows near the roadside the body of the robber. The life for which he had interceded, as he supposed successfully, was after all not his. The Brus with a nod had betrayed the bishop. What wonder that he promptly revoked his blessing and turned it into a curse, first on the Brus and his offspring and second on the town itself.

At some time between 1173 and 1218 catastrophe struck the town of Annan, when it ceased to be the *caput* [capital] of Annandale and was reduced to a mere *vill* [village]. The curiously elongated appearance of the Mote of Annan above the bank of the river indicates a dramatic change in the course of the river which swept away the mote and a substantial part of the accompanying bailey. By 1166 the Brus had established a castle at Lochmaben, sited more conveniently and centrally in Annandale, and it seems probable that the destruction of the fortifications at Annan by natural causes provided the pretext for transferring the administration of the district to Lochmaben or even Dumfries, then beginning to develop as a commercial centre of some importance. As the Lanercost Chronicle puts it, "Annan lost the dignity of a burgh through the curse of a just man."

The effect of St. Malachy's curse on the fortunes of the Bruces

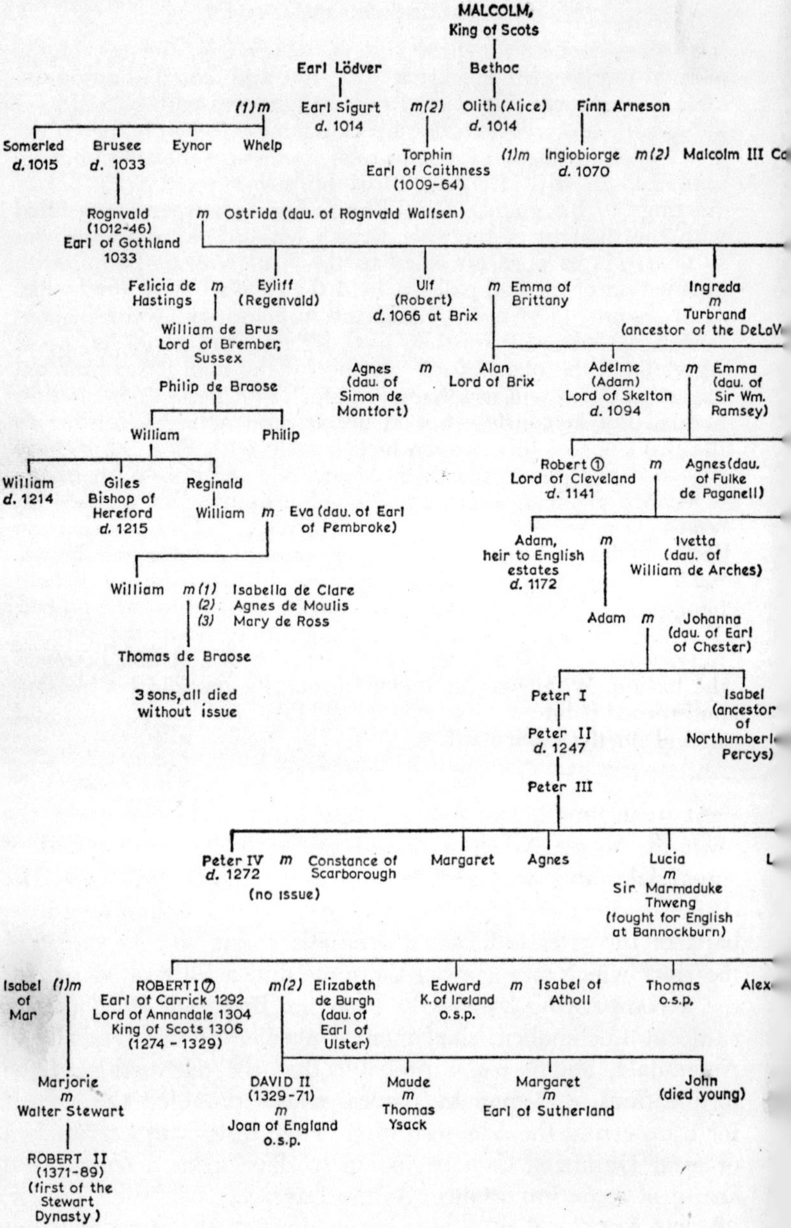

① = First of the name Robert Bruce

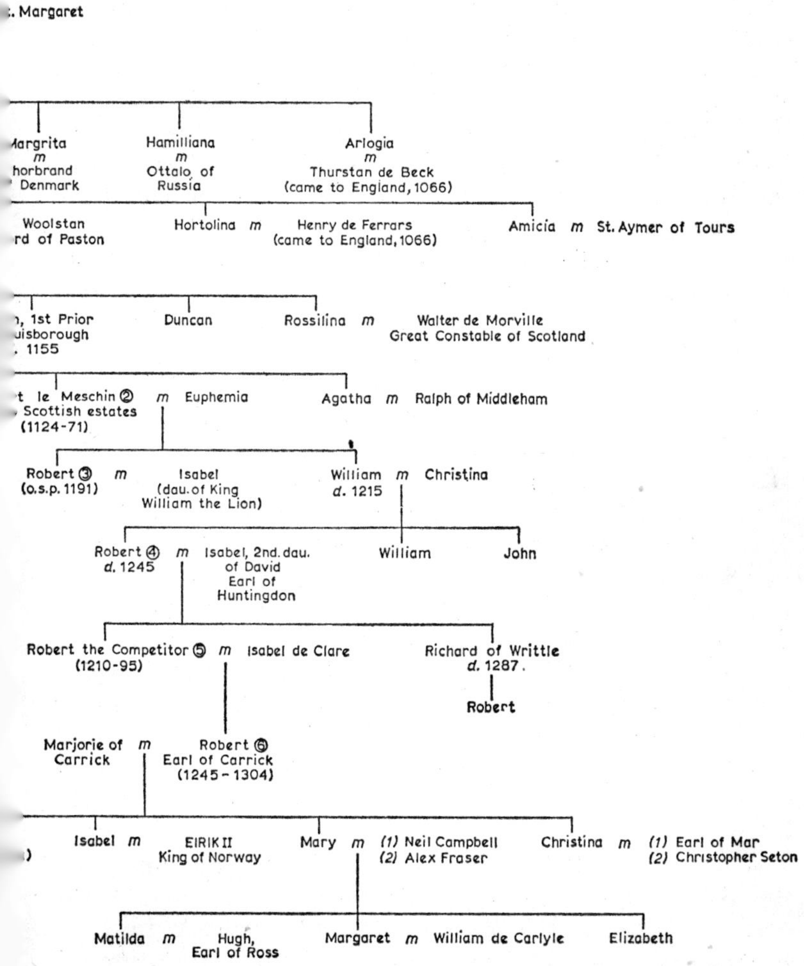

:. Margaret
Aargrita m Thorbrand ' Denmark
Hamilliana m Ottalo of Russia
Arlogia m Thurstan de Beck (came to England, 1066)
Woolstan rd of Paston
Hortolina m Henry de Ferrars (came to England, 1066)
Amicia m St. Aymer of Tours
ı, 1st Prior uisborough . 1155
Duncan
Rossilina m Walter de Morville Great Constable of Scotland
't le Meschin ② m Euphemia
, Scottish estates (1124-71)
Agatha m Ralph of Middleham
Robert ③ m Isabel (dau. of King William the Lion)
(o.s.p. 1191)
William m Christina
d. 1215
Robert ④ m Isabel, 2nd. dau. of David Earl of Huntingdon
d. 1245
William
John
Robert the Competitor ⑤ m Isabel de Clare
(1210-95)
Richard of Writtle
d. 1287.
Robert
Marjorie of Carrick m Robert ⑥ Earl of Carrick (1245-1304)
Isabel m EIRIK II King of Norway
Mary m (1) Neil Campbell (2) Alex Fraser
Christina m (1) Earl of Mar (2) Christopher Seton
Matilda m Hugh, Earl of Ross
Margaret m William de Carlyle
Elizabeth

The Bruce Family and its origin

was less dramatic, but to the unsophisticated medieval mind it was probably no less seriously regarded. It is significant that Robert le Meschin and his wife Euphemia produced only two sons who reached maturity. History has not recorded whether there were other children but it seems likely that there were others who did not survive infancy. The elder son, also named Robert, married Isabel, daughter of King William the Lion, but he died childless in 1191, five years before his father. Little is known of the younger son, William, beyond the facts that he died in 1215 and left three sons—Robert, William and John. The Bruces were keenly aware of the curse and would have been only too ready to attribute any bereavement or mischance to St. Malachy. Almost 130 years after the event the Bruce of that day took positive steps to appease the saint and allay the wrath which had resulted in the curse.

Robert de Brus, the fourth of that name, married Isabel, daughter of David Earl of Huntingdon, the youngest of King David's three grandsons. The two elder grandsons had succeeded him on the Scottish throne—as Malcolm "the Maiden" (1153–65) and William "the Lion" (1165–1214). Isobel of Huntingdon's two elder brothers, Robert and John, died without issue, but her elder sister, Margaret, married Alan of Galloway and their youngest daughter Devorgilla was the mother of John Balliol who later claimed and won the Scottish throne.

The elder son of Robert de Brus and Isabel of Huntingdon was also called Robert. In his early years he was nicknamed the Noble (an epithet applied erroneously by some genealogists and historians to his father), but the nickname which has come down to posterity is The Competitor, of which more will be said later.

Isabel married Robert de Brus in 1209. By the beginning of the thirteenth century the Bruces were ranked among the *Magnates Scotiae,* the great nobility of Scotland. In 1221 Robert, fourth lord of Annandale, was one of the witnesses of the marriage of King Alexander II and Johanna, sister of King Henry III, at York. Isabel was co-heir to her brother John le Scot, last Earl and Count Palatine of Chester. King Henry III felt that the estates of Chester were too great to be entrusted to Isabel so he granted her the manors of Hatfield Broad Oak and Writtle in Essex, as well as half of the Hundred of Harlow, in exchange. She held considerable estates in her own right—Connington in Huntingdon and Exton in Rutland, as well as Garioch and Kildrummie in Scotland. She and her husband preferred to reside on their English estates. Robert had his manor house at Bromeshobury in Hatfield and was styled as lord of Annandale, Writtle and Hatfield, the latter *de jure uxoris.* He himself was a landowner in England of no little importance. His estates included Lamarsh on Stour and the parish of All Saints Tottenham. Bruce Castle in the Greater London borough of Haringey is a reminder to this day of the Bruce connection with Tottenham, though the connection was severed in 1306 when King Robert Bruce forfeited his English estates. The present castle, in fact, dates from 1514 when it was built by Sir William Compton, groom of the bedchamber to King Henry VIII.

Robert the fourth lord died in 1245 and his wife Isabel in 1251. They were buried at Saltre Abbey, Stilton, near the body of David Earl of Huntingdon. On the death of his father Robert the fifth lord of Annandale inherited the Bruce estates and six years later his mother's property also fell to him. By 1252, therefore, he was one of the most important and influential men in either Scotland or England, with estates which included the rapidly developing burgh of Dundee, Hartlepool in County Durham and extensive holdings in Essex. If his aristocratic connections were impeccable, his royal blood was also important. In 1238, according to tradition, he was selected by the childless King Alexander II as his heir, being his nearest male relative. Alexander subsequently married Marie de Couci and produced a son (later Alexander III), but the arrangement of 1238—real or imagined—was to become an important factor in the claim advanced by The Competitor in later years. At any rate the decision of 1238 must have been of short duration, for the birth in that year of Hugh Balliol, the first grandson of the eldest of Earl David's daughters, must have presented a serious challenge to the son of a younger daughter. But, as we shall see later, the law of primogeniture was by no means clearly defined in the thirteenth century.

Robert's career followed the conventional lines of an Anglo-Norman nobleman of the period. Born in 1210 he lived until 1295 and during his long and eventful career he served kings of both England and Scotland. His first steps in the nobility were taken in the thirties; he paid £20 for ten knights' fees which he had of the Honour of Peverell in London and the counties of Essex and Hertford. In May 1240 he married Isabel de Clare, who brought a single manor in Sussex as her dowry, but amply compensated for this in the fact that she was very well connected. Her father was the Earl of Gloucester and her uncle was the Earl Marshal of England. Isabel de Clare gave Robert *entrée* to the innermost establishment circles. In the mid-thirteenth century Robert de Brus took a prominent part in English political life. He was Sheriff of Cumberland and, for some time, Governor of Carlisle Castle. He was for upwards of twenty years a royal judge and became, in 1268, Chief Justice of the Court of King's Bench—the first incumbent of that office. He enjoyed the confidence of the Scottish king in like measure. At the Convention of Roxburgh in 1255 he was appointed Regent of Scotland and a guardian of the youthful Alexander III.

In the constitutional crisis which led to civil war between Henry III and his barons, Robert commanded the Scottish and Cumbrian contingent of men-at-arms supporting the king and his son the Lord Edward at Northampton. When the royalists were decisively defeated by the barons led by Simon de Montford at Lewes, the lord of Annandale, along with his royal masters, was taken prisoner. No quarter was given to the hapless Scots but Bruce himself was spared and subsequently released on payment of a substantial ransom.

That Robert the Noble was a man of his time is shown in his enthusiasm to go on a crusade. In 1269 he set out for the Holy Land, accompanying the Lord Edmund (Henry III's younger son) on an expedition mounted by King Louis of France against the Soldan of Tunis. Subsequently he travelled all over the Near and Middle East, accompanied by his son Robert, his brother Richard of Writtle (and *his* son Robert) and the Lord Edward (later King Edward I). The unimaginative repetition of the name Robert in the Bruce family is confusing. There is a reference to a Robert de Brus, whom King Edward I described as "*dilectus bachelarius noster*" (our delightful bachelor), to whom he lent £40. Dalrymple (*Annals*) and Douglas (*Peerage*) both mistook this for the son of Robert the Noble, but it seems more probable that it was Robert, son of Richard de Brus, to whom the king referred.

To Robert the Noble is given credit for lifting the curse of St. Malachy. As the Lanercost Chronicle states,

> On coming to manhood he personally went to the saint [i.e. the saint's tomb], craved his pardon, commended himself to him, and thereafter visited the saint every three years. Moreover, returning in his later days (1272–3) from pilgrimage in the Holy Land where he had been with Sir Edward (later Edward I), he turned aside to Clairvaux and there for ever made his peace with the saint and provided a perpetual rent from which three silver lamps with their lights are maintained on the saint's tomb.

This story is confirmed by a charter, preserved at Clairvaux, which states:

> Charter of Robert de Brus, lord of Annandale, granting to God and the Blessed Mary and to the house and monks of Clairvaux, in order to maintain lights before the blessed Malachy and for the good of his own soul and the souls of his predecessors and successors, the lands of Osticroft as Roger de ——, William de Wode and Galfrid Collan lately held of the granter, free of all multures at the granters mill and free of all secular customs and services. Wit – Sir David de Torthorwald then steward of Annandale, Sir Richard de Herice [Herries] and Sir William de Saint Michael knights, Mr Adam de Kirkcudbricht, Dom. William de Duncorry, William de Corri, Adam Hendeman, Richard Crispin and William de Are [Ayr].

The above mentioned lands of Osticroft have not been identified. Some historians, in light of subsequent events, have tended to place too much significance on this act of piety, suggesting almost that Robert was anticipating his subsequent aspirations to the throne by eliminating the malediction which might stand in his way. Others more cautiously say that we can only guess at Bruce's reasons for wishing so strongly for reconciliation. There may, indeed, have been no real reason, or he may merely have wished to propitiate the saint before announcing his second marriage, which took place in May 1273 to Christiana de Ireby, daughter of a neighbour in Cumberland, William de Ireby. Christiana was a widow twice over and for obscure reasons the Bruce's family resented the match. Bruce's son tried without success to withhold his stepmother's dower on the grounds that her marriage to his father was unlawful, but he was overruled by a decision in the Court of King's Bench. By his second marriage Robert the Noble acquired the manors of Great Baddon in Essex and Kemston in Bedfordshire.

By his first wife Robert the Noble had a son whom he called Robert. The younger Bruce was born in 1245 and, unlike his energetic father, is a shadowy figure about whom little is known. At best he is something of an enigma, playing an equivocal part in the turbulent events from 1286 onwards; at worst he seemed singularly lacking in those characteristics which marked his father and his son. One historian has described him as spineless and colourless; another has gone so far as to call him " the other Empty Jacket " (on the same analogy as King John Balliol). These judgments are, perhaps, too harsh and facile. He was widely-travelled for his time. In later life his son-in-law was the King of Norway and he is known to have spent some time at that court. He was also more interested in the management of his English estates than the often unseemly squabbling over the Scottish throne and he may have seen the wheeling and dealing of late thirteenth-century Anglo-Scottish politics in their true light. At most, it was his misfortune to come between the Competitor Bruce and Bruce the King. While he lived he was something of an embarrassment to his son who could not very well advance his own claims so long as his father had the better claim—and cared little about it.

When he was 24 he accompanied his father, uncle and cousin on crusade and returned safely from that disastrous expedition in 1272 or 1273. One of his companions in arms was Adam de Kilconquhar, great-grandson of Duncan Earl of Fife. Adam was slain at the siege of Acre and tradition has it that Robert de Brus brought news of his death to Adam's young bride, Marjorie, Countess of Carrick in her own right.

The Countess Marjorie was the last of her line. Her father, Neil, Earl of Carrick, held extensive lands in Ayrshire and was the last direct male descendant of Fergus of Galloway, a Celtic prince who wielded virtually sovereign power in the south-west in the days of King David I. Marjorie's father died in 1256, when she was a baby, and this great Celtic earldom had passed to her. She was little more than a child when she was wed to Adam and he departed for the Holy Land shortly afterwards—

though not before Marjorie had conceived. The child of this ephemeral marriage was a girl who later was to marry Thomas Randolph, Earl of Moray, a staunch supporter of Robert Bruce.

A great deal of romantic nonsense has been talked and written about the courtship of the younger de Brus and the Countess Marjorie, the substance of which is that, having delivered his sad tidings, he was playfully arrested by Marjorie's attendants and escorted to her castle of Turnberry where, after a brief but hectic courtship, they were married. It is said that King Alexander III was displeased at the match, and a fine was imposed on the young couple before the royal displeasure was abated. By the application of feudal law Marjorie would have been regarded as a royal ward on account of her widowhood and noble birth, and a fee would normally be payable to the king on the event of her remarriage. It is hardly likely that the king would have objected to a marriage which united a close kinsman with one of the oldest and most powerful (and potentially most troublesome) Celtic families of the kingdom.

Today little remains of Turnberry Castle but its foundations and a few fragments of walls, but what remains is remarkable enough, owing to its situation. The castle perches on a cliff overlooking the Firth of Clyde and the mountains of Arran and Kintyre. The sea has scored deep gashes into the face of the cliff and these natural features were incorporated into the defences of the castle. Sufficient stretches of solid masonry survive to indicate the impregnability of this sea-girt fastness. On the landward side it is less impressive, though formerly it may have possessed a fine appearance. Clearly the *caput* of the earldom of Carrick was intended primarily for the defence of the fertile farmlands of Ayrshire against attack from the sea. Only a decade prior to the meeting of Marjorie and Robert, Alexander III had defeated the Norse under Haco at Largs farther up the coast and the menace of attack from Norway was not eliminated till 1266 when a treaty between Norway and Scotland was sealed by the marriage of Alexander's daughter Margaret and Haco's son Eirik.

Robert became Earl of Carrick as a result of his marriage. As one of the thirteen earls of Scotland he now outranked his father, though such was the difference in their temperament and character that this fact seldom, if ever, counted. The true significance of this marriage was political—an important link between the ancient Celtic Scotland and the new Anglo-Norman Scotland. Paradoxically Marjorie could count a king of England among her ancestors; Fergus's wife was one of the innumerable bastard progeny of Henry I. And Robert was the great-great-great-great grandson of Malcolm Canmore, the last truly Celtic king of Scotland.

From Turnberry one looks out over the firth to Ailsa Craig. Today it is jocularly known as Paddy's Milestone, because of its position midway between Glasgow and Belfast. In a way it also symbolizes the fact that the earls of Carrick were as much preoccupied with Ireland as with Scotland and had close connections with the Irish aristocracy. Conversely there were also long-standing animosities and rivalry between Carrick and Galloway proper (modern Wigtownshire and the Stewartry of Kirkcudbright) and this factor played no small part in the relationships between the Bruces and the other great magnates of Scotland around the turn of the century. This hostility, amounting at times to blood feud, arose from the quarrels of Gilbert and Uhtred, the sons of Fergus of Galloway. Uhtred was brutally put to death at Gilbert's behest and Gilbert, in turn, had been dispossessed of the Galloway lands by Uhtred's heirs and avengers. The great granddaughters of Gilbert and Uhtred were respectively Marjorie of Carrick and Devorgilla Balliol.

On 11th July, 1274 the Countess of Carrick gave birth to a son, the seventh of his line to be named Robert. Curiously enough, although the exact date of his birth is known the actual place of birth is the subject of controversy. Turnberry, Lochmaben and even Writtle in Essex have been put forward for that honour. We can safely dismiss the last of these since the sole authority for an English birthplace was the chronicler Geoffrey le Baker of Swinbrook whose writings contain the astonishing statement that King Alexander III of Scotland had no sons but three daughters who married John Balliol, John Comyn and Robert Bruce respectively. Robert is referred to as "English by birth, born in Essex". The statement about Alexander's daughters is so palpably untrue that one immediately suspects anything else in this chronicle. It is not impossible that Robert, Earl of Carrick was born at Writtle, but it seems more likely that Geoffrey le Baker had confused his Robert de Brus with that Robert de Brus, son of Richard de Brus of Writtle and nephew of Robert the Noble. On the other hand, the near-contemporary Guisborough Chronicle quotes Robert Bruce (the future king) as referring to Scotland as his native country. One might also cite the preamble to the Harcla Treaty of 1323 which alludes to the fact that England (under Edward II) and Scotland (under Robert I) each had a king of its own nation.

If the claim of Writtle may be safely dismissed, the dispute between Turnberry and Lochmaben is less easily settled. Lochmaben was fortified by the Bruces about 1166 and sometime thereafter, as has already been noted, the *caput* of Annandale was transferred to that place from Annan. Throughout the thirteenth century the lords of Annandale governed the district from a mote erected on what is still called Castlehill. Nearby is the site of the medieval church and it was here, on the ridge separating the Kirk Loch from the Castle Loch, that the township of Lochmaben developed. In 1274 this was the home of Robert the Noble and it seems more probable that his son, the Earl of Carrick, would have taken up residence at Turnberry. No documentary evidence exists in support of Lochmaben's claim. This rests merely on oral tradition which, in turn, may have arisen out of the vague assumption that, as Lochmaben was the seat of the lords of Annandale, it necessarily followed that Robert the future king was born there. King Robert is portrayed proudly on the burgh arms and the Latin motto "*E nobis liberator rex*" (from us is sprung the liberator king) alludes to the claim; but the arms and motto are of seventeenth-century origin and date back no farther than 1612 when King James VI granted a written charter re-affirming the ancient privileges bestowed by King Robert in the early fourteenth century. Today the memory of the town's most illustrious son is kept alive by a late Victorian statue, a stained glass window in the Town Hall (of the same vintage), Bruce Street, the Bruce Arms Hotel and sundry trades and businesses which exploit the name Bruce in their title.

Turnberry, on the other hand, has done nothing to maintain the memory of the liberator king. No sign, no stone, no memorial are to be found in that locality to acquaint the casual passer-by—yet the oral tradition of Bruce's birth is just as strong as that of Lochmaben, and, in view of the circumstances of the time, it seems logical to regard the Turnberry tradition as the stronger of the two.

Marjorie bore her husband a large family—five sons and six daughters. Of the sons, Robert alone was to die in his bed; three of them perished on English scaffolds and a fourth was killed in battle. Two of the sons became kings and one daughter, by marriage, became a queen.

Of the boyhood of Robert Bruce nothing is known. It is assumed that sometime after his twelfth birthday, in July 1286, he entered page's service at Turnberry. The Paisley Registrum contains a deed of Alexander Macdonald of Islay, witnessed by the Earl of Carrick and his eldest son, among others, and it seems as though he entered into the affairs of the earldom about this time.

And then, on 19th March of that year, King Alexander III of Scotland was killed in a riding accident at Pettycur promontory on the cliffs near Kinghorn in Fife.

CHAPTER II

A Kingdom without a King

MONDAY, 18TH MARCH 1286 was a wild, stormy day in the east of Scotland, with more than a hint of snow in the air and equinoctial gales raging round the coast. It was a day beset by evil omens, and strange rumours that it would be the Day of Judgment. More specifically a prophet had warned the king that his horse would be the death of him. He solved this problem by having the poor creature put to death. Later a story gained credence that it was the sight of this beast's skeleton which had frightened the king's steed into rearing up and throwing the hapless rider over the cliffs. This is no more than a colourful fable, but it does capture the spirit of the time.

The facts of the matter are fairly well documented. The king held his council at Edinburgh that day, dined late with his advisers and then, seemingly on impulse, decided to return to his residence at Kinghorn on the other side of the Firth of Forth, where his young bride, Yolande of Dreux, lay waiting her master's pleasure. Alexander was then a man in the prime of life, four years older than the Earl of Carrick. He had succeeded his father, Alexander II, in 1249 when he was eight years old, but during an effective reign spanning almost thirty years he had unified Scotland, eliminated many of the old, traditional rivalries, consolidated the feudalization begun under David I and beaten off the menace from the North. In true medieval fashion he had assured the position of his country by marriage. His first wife, Margaret, was an English princess. After her death he married again, choosing a French noblewoman, forerunner of a long line of French princesses and aristocrats whose marriage with Scottish kings cemented the ties between France and Scotland. His only daughter, Margaret, had married Eirik II of Norway.

Tragedy struck the Scottish royal house in the eighties. David, Alexander's younger son, died in 1281 and Alexander, the elder son, died three years later. Margaret of Norway died in childbirth, leaving as heir to the Scottish and Norwegian thrones a girl baptized Margaret but more commonly known to history as the Maid of Norway. After Prince Alexander's death the sorrowing king took steps to have his baby granddaughter acknowledged by the magnates of Scotland as his successor. The following year, in 1285, he remarried, and the hopes of Scotland were pinned on his French bride presenting him with a son or sons to ensure the continuation of the dynasty.

Ignoring the advice of his counsellors Alexander set out from Edinburgh that stormy night, braved the perilous crossing of the firth from Dalmeny to Inverkeithing, where he was met by Alexander le Saucier, master of the royal sauce-kitchen and a bailie of the burgh. The saucier bluntly asked the king, " My lord, what are you doing out in such weather and darkness? How many times have I tried to persuade you that midnight travelling will bring you no good? " The last remark seems to imply that the king was in the habit of commuting nocturnally between Edinburgh and his royal manor. The king turned down the offer of hospitality and ignored the warning, and with an escort of three esquires and two local guides, set off for his house at Kinghorn. Eleven miles of indescribably bad road lay between Inverkeithing and Kinghorn. Not far from their destination the king became separated from his companions in the pitchblack night, took a wrong turning and ended up on the cliffs of Pettycur. The exact manner of his death will never be known, but his body with a broken neck was found among the rocks at the foot of the cliffs the following day. Yolande had not conceived, so the succession of the throne devolved on a sickly three-year-old in a distant land across the northern seas.

Scotland in 1286 was a vastly different place from the present-day country. It lacked the Orkney and Shetland Islands, both administered by Denmark until 1468 when they passed to Scotland as part of the dowry of the wife of King James III, but included the Isle of Man, acquired from Norway in 1266, along with the Western Isles. Berwick was then a Scottish city of considerable commercial and strategic importance. The largest town was Edinburgh while Glasgow was relatively unimportant but for its cathedral. Much of the land was thickly covered with forest, the haunt of wolves and wild boar. The human population was less than a tenth of its present size. Not till 1500 did it pass the half-million mark, doubled again in the ensuing two centuries and only rose rapidly from the beginning of the nineteenth century onwards. It was still essentially a Celtic country, and Gaelic was the everyday language north of the Forth and Clyde and also in Galloway. English, of a sort, was spoken in much of the Lowlands, but Norman-French was the tongue of the upper classes. Norse would still be understood in the Western Isles and even parts of Caithness and Sutherland and there were important colonies of Flemings and other northern Europeans in the seaports and trading centres, especially along the east coast. Scotland as a country still barely existed, and the Scots as a nation had only acquired an identity almost within living memory. The term Scotia, previously used to designate the land north of Clyde and Forth, was only applied to the whole of the kingdom in the reign of Alexander III.

The reign of Alexander III had been one of peace and prosperity for Scotland. The settled condition of the country for much of the thirteenth century encouraged the development of industry based on an agricultural economy. There was a thriving export trade, in fish, timber, wool and hides, to the Low Countries, Germany and Scandinavia as well as to northern England and Ireland. Economically, socially and culturally Scotland was orientated towards the mainland of northern Europe rather than towards her more powerful southern neighbour. After the Battle of Largs and the treaty of 1266 relations between Scotland and the Norse countries improved rapidly—a fact which is often overlooked.

The relationship between Scotland and England, however, was none too clearly defined. Overlordship was the paramount factor in the feudal system which was beginning to appear in England long before the Norman Conquest but was perfected in the years following 1066. As far back as Edgar in 973 there was a claim by the Wessex kings to be the overlords or superiors of their northern neighbours. A century later, in 1072, William the Conqueror invaded Scotland in retaliation against raids by Malcolm Canmore (who married the sister of Edgar the Atheling). In the chronicler's vague phrase Malcolm became William's man, making his submission to the Norman at Abernethy. That Malcolm attached little importance to this is borne out by subsequent events; Malcolm ravaged the north of England in 1079 and 1091. After the latter raid William Rufus invaded Scotland as his father had done twenty years earlier, and wrung from Malcolm a second admission of homage, with the added proviso that Malcolm should hasten to him whenever his feudal superior should demand his attendance. Thenceforward Malcolm's successors were virtually vassals of the English king. Paradoxically it was only after David, Earl of Huntingdon and Northampton, became King of Scots in 1124 that the Scottish monarch began once more to assert his own sovereignty, and the weakness of England after the death of Henry I in 1135 allowed this assertion to go unchecked.

It was only after the accession of Henry II in 1154 that the relationship of the Scottish king was called into question. Scotland herself had had a new king only the previous year, a twelve year-old boy known to posterity as Malcolm the Maiden on account of his effeminate appearance and weak character. Malcolm IV was no match for the strong-willed Henry. Beset by the opposition and rebelliousness of the Celtic north and Galloway Malcolm turned more and more to Henry for help, and, in return, was forced to acknowledge English patronage. In 1159 he fought in the English army in an expedition against the French at Toulouse and was knighted by the English king. His brother and successor, William the Lion (1165–1214) was a man of different mettle. Though he and his younger brother David, together with the Scottish barons, did homage to Henry II at Easter 1170, he was only biding his time for an opportunity to assert his independence. In the summer of 1174 he took the field with an army which ravaged the northern counties of England but by a stroke of ill-luck was captured near Alnwick and swiftly conveyed to Falaise in Normandy where a humiliating treaty was extorted from him. William not only agreed to become Henry's vassal for the whole of his kingdom, north as well as south of the Forth, but had to allow the English to garrison the castles of Berwick, Edinburgh, Jedburgh, Roxburgh and Stirling. Furthermore his brother David and twenty-one of the leading Scottish barons were handed over to the English as hostages. David was well-treated and was later created Earl of Huntingdon, spending the rest of his life as an English magnate. He it was whose three daughters were the mother or grandmothers of claimants to the Scottish throne.

The accession of Richard the Lionheart in 1189 brought a change to Anglo-Scottish relations. Richard was more interested in crusading in the Holy Land and with a view to raising the money to finance an expedition he restored the independence of Scotland and withdrew his garrisons for the relatively paltry sum of 10,000 marks. Theoretically the status quo of 1174 was restored, but what precisely had been the relationship of William the Lion to King Henry before the Treaty of Falaise was never defined. The situation was clouded by the fact that the kings of Scotland held extensive estates in England whereas the kings of England never held land in Scotland. Thus, at each coronation in England the Scottish king was required to do homage for his English estates and as this practice was never reciprocated the belief that the king of England was somehow superior gained strength. Significantly it was Alexander III, following the accession of Edward I in 1277, who tried to define the position more clearly. On 29th October 1278 he did homage to Edward saying, "I become your man for the lands which I hold of you in the kingdom of England for which I owe homage, saving my kingdom." William Middleton, Bishop of Norwich, interjected, "And be it saved to the king of England if he have a right to homage for it." To which Alexander riposted, "No one has a right to homage for my kingdom of Scotland save God alone, and I hold it only of God."

While the kings of England sought their brides on the Continent the kings of Scotland had brides imposed on them from England. One cannot place overmuch significance on this in itself; it was probably quite logical for English princesses to become Scottish queens, and this custom had been going on since Malcolm Canmore took the saintly Margaret of the old Anglo-Saxon dynasty as his wife. More significantly the Scottish kings of the thirteenth century began to look elsewhere for their brides. Alexander II's first wife had been Joan, sister of Henry

III; but when she died childless Alexander chose Marie de Couci, great-great-granddaughter of Louis VI of France. Alexander III, half-French by birth, likewise chose a French lady as his second wife, Yolande of Dreux, another descendant of Louis VI. In these marriages lay the seeds of the Auld Alliance which flourished between Scotland and France in the fifteenth and sixteenth centuries. But the untimely death of Alexander III brought this incipient French influence to an abrupt end.

Had Yolande produced a son and posthumous heir to Alexander all might have been well, and there were strong rumours of the young queen's pregnancy. But this turned out to be wishful thinking. A fortnight after Easter 1286, or little more than a month after Alexander's death, the magnates of Scotland and the leading clergy met at Scone near Perth and took the oath of fealty to their sovereign lady, Margaret of Norway, and solemnly swore to protect and uphold the peace of the land. That done, they set up a form of provisional government, appointing six *custodes pacis* (Guardians of the Peace) as regents. The Guardians consisted of two earls, Alexander Comyn of Buchan and Duncan of Fife, two barons James the Steward and John Comyn of Badenoch, and two bishops, Robert Wishart of Glasgow and William Fraser of St. Andrews. The earls and Bishop Fraser had special responsibility for Scotland north of the Forth, the barons and Bishop Wishart for the southern districts. The earls of Buchan and Fife were the most powerful landowners in the north; the Steward was the principal officer of the royal household and held extensive lands in the south-west of Scotland, while Comyn of Badenoch, despite his title, had important estates in the Border counties. Significantly the selection of the Guardians avoided any controversial figure, such as Bruce of Annandale or John Balliol who were related to the royal house and might have a claim to the throne in place of the Maid of Norway.

The Guardians also considered it prudent to contact King Edward I, then campaigning in Gascony, keeping him informed of the situation. The mission seems to have been to seek Edward's advice and assistance rather than to acknowledge his overlordship—though this embassy was seen in retrospect to indicate Edward's superiority.

In the dangerous political vacuum created by the death of the king and the minority of his distant granddaughter, the Guardians were at pains to emphasize that they had been elected by common counsel or the community of the realm. Inevitably there were some who held other views about the future of the country and were not content to acknowledge the sovereignty of some remote baby princess. Already the aspirations of John Balliol and Robert Bruce were being publicized and opinion, in the south-west at least, was polarizing round these two powerful barons. Sometime in the summer of 1286 the lord of Annandale took steps to minimize potential opposition. He and his son, the Earl of Carrick, mustered an armed force, seized the Balliol stronghold of Buittle and the royal castles of Dumfries and Wigtown. The precise reasons for this attack are obscure but in the context of the times the motives of the Bruce family seem clear enough. Possession of Dumfries castle gave the Bruces control over the route through Nithsdale to their lands in Carrick and, by the same token, contained the Balliols in Galloway. In John Balliol's Pleas for the Crown there appears the following description of the Bruces' action.

> The aforesaid Sir Robert de Brus and the Earl of Karrick, his son, dared to take by force of arms with banners displayed the aforesaid Lady of Scotland's castle of Dumfries, against her peace. And thence the aforesaid Sir Robert advanced to the castle of Botil, and there he caused one Patrick MacCuffok within the bailey of the same castle to proclaim that all the —— [unintelligible in the original document] should immediately depart from the land. The Earl of Karrick with the assent and power of his father took the aforesaid Lady's Castle of Wigton in Galloway, and killed many of her men there.

On 20th September 1286 a group of noblemen which included one of the Guardians, James the Steward, the Bruces father and son and the lord of Islay, met at the seat of the Earl of Carrick and entered into a band or sworn agreement to give aid to Thomas de Clare and the Earl of Ulster, Richard de Burgh against their enemies. The Turnberry Band may have been occasioned by no more than some vague Irish adventure, though many historians have asserted (on insufficient evidence) that the Band upheld Bruce's claims to the throne. In fact they took an oath saving the fealty of all parties to the king of

England and "to whoever shall be king of Scotland by reason of the blood of the late King Alexander"—which seems to imply the hypothetical son of the supposedly pregnant Yolande.

The Guardians issued a writ to sheriffs and other royal officers to mobilize knights, freemen and others who owed military service to the royal dignity for the defence of the realm and there is some evidence that levies were in fact called out in the spring of 1287. But by that time the revolt of the Turnberry Band—if it was indeed a revolt—had fizzled out and the south-west was restored to its former tranquillity. Nevertheless the meeting of September 1286 left an ugly taste in the mouth; the Guardians lacked solidarity and powerful magnates like the Bruces seemed inclined to disregard such notions as the community of the realm whenever it suited their purpose.

Apart from the Turnberry incident and the actions of the Bruces which led up to it, the history of Scotland from 1286 to 1290 was relatively uneventful. In 1289 Alexander Comyn died of old age, but in September of that year the Earl of Fife, whom the Lanercost Chronicle describes as cruel and greedy above the average, was murdered by his own family. The earls were thus left unrepresented, though in some respects Bishop Matthew Crambeth of Dunkeld and Sir Andrew Murray of Petty seem to have been co-opted in place of the deceased Guardians. Meanwhile negotiations were in progress for the marriage of the Maid of Norway to the Lord Edward, son of Edward I and a year her junior. These negotations culminated in the Treaty of Birgham on 18th July 1290, ratified by Edward I at Northampton a month later.

That this was to be a union of two people rather than a union of two countries was clearly emphasized in the terms laid down by the Guardians. Edward and Margaret might become one flesh, but Scotland and England were to remain separate.

In October 1289 the Guardians decided that the time had come for the Maid of Norway to take possession of her kingdom. Three of the Guardians—Bishops Wishart and Fraser and John Comyn of Badenoch—together with Bruce of Annandale were despatched to treat with commissioners of Norway and England regarding Margaret's return and prospective marriage. The three groups of commissioners reached an amicable arrangement and presented their reports to King Edward at Salisbury

(*right*) Statue of William Wallace at the entrance to Edinburgh Castle; (*below*) The Wallace Memorial near Stirling

(*above*) Stirling Castle; (*below*) Glen Trool. The stone commemorating the battle of 1307 is in the centre of the picture

on 9th November. The terms were agreed as follows. Margaret was to come over to England or Scotland by All Saints Day (1st November) 1290. She was to come free of any prior marriage contract. Edward I was to be given assurances that she would not be married except by his ordinance, will and counsel, and that Scotland was in a safe and peaceful condition, so that Margaret might live there willingly " as its true lady, queen and heir ". The Scots reserved the right, however, to remove any unsuitable guardians or servants supplied by Norway and replace them by Scots who were to be approved by men of both countries and by King Edward's agents. In these and other matters the arbitration of Edward was sought as a matter of course.

At the same time Pope Nicholas IV issued a bull granting dispensation for the marriage of the two cousins, King Edward having put forward the plea that it was a matter of political necessity that Margaret should be married to his son. From correspondence in March 1290 it was clear that the Scots, on their side, welcomed the marriage. At this time they wrote to Eirik II formally asking his acceptance of the match, and at the same time they wrote to prince Edward referring to " the joyous tidings of which many people speak "—an allusion to the papal bull of dispensation.

On the English side the chief architect of the Treaty of Birgham was Antony Bek, prince-bishop of Durham, a leading prelate and a powerful magnate. For some time previously the bishop had been Edward's chief agent in Scottish and Norwegian affairs. In February 1290 King Edward had appointed him custodian of the Scottish monarch's estates in Penrith and Tynedale. In June he was empowered to admit to the king's peace the men of the Scottish Islands " who were in war and discord ". In August Edward asked the remaining Guardians of Scotland to recognize the bishop as the lieutenant in Scotland of Margaret and her husband and to defer to him in all matters " which are required for the governance and peaceful state of the realm ".

The terms of the Treaty of Birgham explicitly preserved the independence of Scotland " separate, free and without subjection ". Tenants-in-chief were required to do homage in Scotland alone, no court outwith the kingdom could have jurisdiction over persons in Scotland, neither York nor Canterbury could interfere in the elections of the Scots clergy. The legal framework of Scotland was to be preserved intact and no writ of common law or letter of special favour could be issued other than by the normal process of the 'king's chapel' and of the Scottish realm. Other clauses limited the rights of any parliament other than that of Scotland to legislate for, or impose taxes on, the Scots. The Treaty of Birgham was a canny document; the Guardians did their best to protect their country's interests, both for the present and, as far as they could foresee, for the future. There was one disquieting event which seems, however, to have excited little comment or foreboding at the time. Early in June 1290 Edward I quietly installed Walter Huntercombe as governor of the Isle of Man and effectively made the island an English protectorate. As if to give this action retrospective legality the Manxmen submitted a petition to Edward saying that they were in need of his protection. Edward's takeover seemed oddly at variance with his reasonable attitude towards Scotland at this time. Nevertheless he had, in effect, seized an important part of the Scottish realm—an island which was strategically important to England and Ireland as well as Scotland.

Meanwhile the practical details of the queen's 'homecoming' were settled. King Edward fitted out a ship for the express purpose of bringing the girl-queen over from Norway. The victualling of the ship was meticulous, including sweetmeats, fruit and two stone of gingerbread. The ship arrived in Norway in May 1290, but returned to England a month later, empty-handed. Eirik decided to send his daughter to Scotland via the northern isles which then formed a part of his kingdom, and it was in Orkney that envoys of the Scottish community were to meet their queen at the beginning of October. Meanwhile the magnates of Scotland assembled at Perth to meet the bishop of Durham, the Earl Warenne and the Dean of York. Subsequently the English mission, with Bishop Fraser of St. Andrews, made the arduous journey north to Orkney.

On 9th October Bishop Fraser wrote to Edward from Leuchars saying that there was a rumour of the queen's death and that he feared civil war would be the outcome unless Edward took steps to prevent it. The letter went on to hint that

John Balliol might go to Edward, and Fraser urged the king to handle him carefully " so that your honour and advantage may be preserved ". The closing remarks of the letter made the worthy bishop's views clear. He urged Edward to come up to the Border, to be ready to install the rightful heir " if so be he will follow your counsel ".

The generally accepted story is that Queen Margaret turned ill on the voyage from Norway to Orkney and died soon after landing there, on 26th September. Her corpse was returned to her sorrowing father at Bergen—and thus the ancient Scottish dynasty finally and tragically came to an end.

Chapter III

The Great Cause

Scotland's problem, following the death of the Maid of Norway, was not a lack of an heir to the throne but too many heirs. In all, thirteen candidates came forward, most of them basing their claims on descent, legitimately or illegitimately from the Scottish royal house. Eirik II claimed the Scottish throne, in right of his late wife and daughter. Had his wife lived after Alexander III he would have had a strong claim *de jure uxoris,* but her untimely decease made his candidature frivolous. John of Badenoch, the Black Comyn, put forward a claim based on descent from Donald Ban, younger brother of Malcolm Canmore. Despite his tenuous link with the royal family the Black Comyn could back up his claim with the fact that he was one of the most powerful men in the land, a Guardian of Scotland and closely connected with the Earls of Buchan and Mar. Seven of the claimants were descended from royal bastards, one the illegitimate offspring of Alexander II, five from William the Lion and one from Henry of Scotland, son of David I. As illegitimacy was regarded, even then, as a strong bar to inheritance, none of these claims could be seriously entertained.

Of the five legitimate descendants of David I one, oddly enough, did not bother to enter a claim. John II, Duke of Brittany, was a great-great-grandson of Margaret, younger sister of David Earl of Huntingdon, by her marriage to Conon of Brittany. At best it would have been a weak claim, but in an age when the laws of primogeniture were by no means clearly defined, it was a claim worth making. Incidentally, John's son

Arthur II subsequently married Yolande of Dreux, the young widow of Alexander III. Ada, elder sister of David of Huntingdon, married Florence III (or Florent III), Count of Holland, and her great-grandson, Florence V, was one of the four legitimate claimants. The other three were the descendants of David of Huntingdon himself, through his three daughters, Margaret, Isobel and Ada. The claimants were, respectively, John Balliol, grandson of the eldest daughter, Robert Bruce of Annandale, son of Isobel, and John Hastings of Abergavenny, grandson of the youngest daughter. It should also be pointed out that Devorgilla, mother of John Balliol, was the youngest daughter of Margaret. The eldest daughter of Margaret was Elena and her daughter Isabella married Alexander Comyn, Earl of Buchan, the father (by a previous marriage) of John Comyn who claimed the throne.

For all practical purposes, however, the dispute resolved itself around Balliol and Bruce. By the law of primogeniture Balliol had the stronger claim, but the precedence of the grandson of an elder sister over the son of a younger sister was not clearly established. Whether Robert Bruce actually believed that he had the stronger claim is immaterial; he certainly acted as though this were the case, re-inforced by the claim that he had been nominated as heir to Alexander II fifty years earlier when the succession, on a previous occasion, had not seemed secure. While the death of Margaret was still no more than a rumour the lord of Annandale and his henchmen assembled under arms and marched on Perth—a fact which Bishop Fraser was quick to point out to King Edward in that famous letter of 7th October.

At this point Edward's wife, Eleanor of Castile, died and any action he proposed taking was delayed by the period of mourning. In retrospect it can be seen that Edward was primarily concerned about maintaining law and order in Scotland rather than backing a claimant who would be pliant to his will, but fundamentally he was anxious to use the leaderless condition of Scotland to advance his own position as feudal overlord of the northern kingdom. It has to be conceded that Balliol was legally the right choice for the throne, and in this aspect Edward acted as impartially as an arbitrator should, but in every other sense Edward acted unfairly and high-handedly.

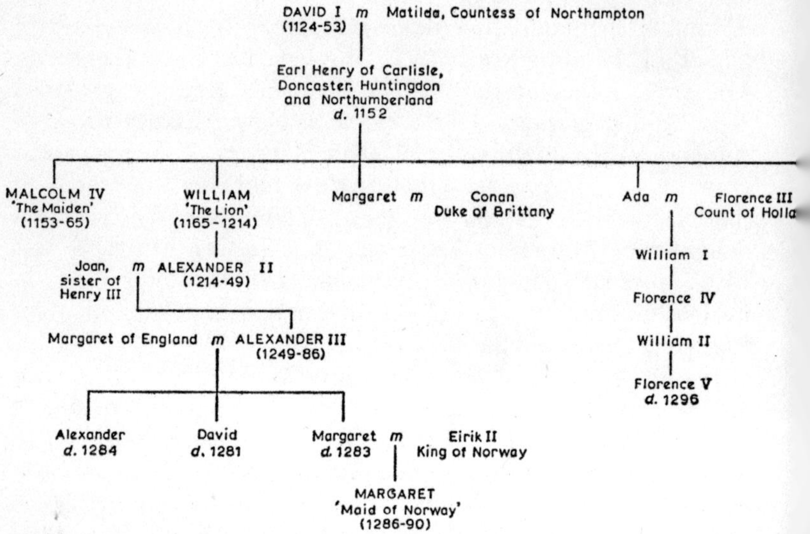
DAVID I m Matilda, Countess of Northampton
(1124-53)
Earl Henry of Carlisle, Doncaster, Huntingdon and Northumberland
d. 1152
MALCOLM IV
'The Maiden'
(1153-65)
WILLIAM
'The Lion'
(1165-1214)
Margaret m Conan
Duke of Brittany
Ada m Florence III
Count of Holla
Joan, sister of Henry III m ALEXANDER II
(1214-49)
William I
Florence IV
William II
Florence V
d. 1296
Margaret of England m ALEXANDER III
(1249-86)
Alexander
d. 1284
David
d. 1281
Margaret m Eirik II
d. 1283
King of Norway
MARGARET
'Maid of Norway'
(1286-90)

Claimants to the Scottish throne 1290–92

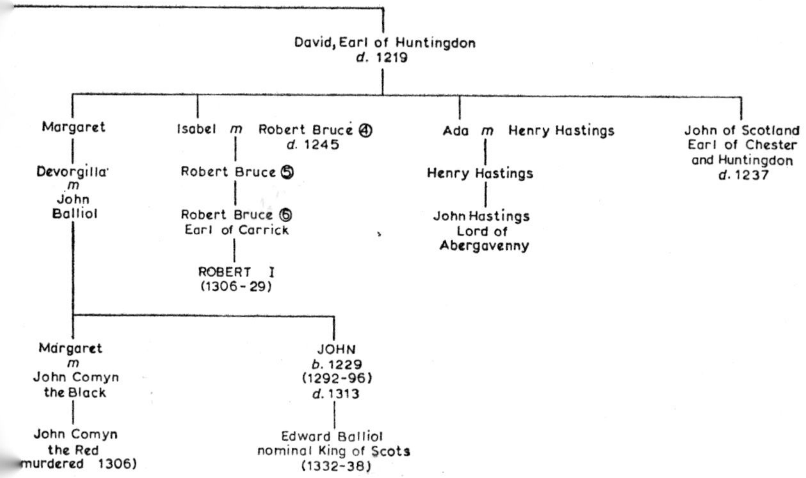
David, Earl of Huntingdon
d. 1219
Margaret
Devorgilla
m
John
Balliol
Isabel m Robert Bruce ④
d. 1245
Robert Bruce ⑤
Robert Bruce ⑥
Earl of Carrick
ROBERT I
(1306-29)
Ada m Henry Hastings
Henry Hastings
John Hastings
Lord of
Abergavenny
John of Scotland
Earl of Chester
and Huntingdon
d. 1237
Margaret
m
John Comyn
the Black
John Comyn
the Red
murdered 1306)
JOHN
b. 1229
(1292-96)
d. 1313
Edward Balliol
nominal King of Scots
(1332-38)

In May 1291 Edward hurried north to Antony Bek's castle at Norham on Tweed and from there issued an assurance to the Guardians and other leading Scots that if they came to negotiate with him he would not put them at a disadvantage by virtue of their crossing the Tweed to the English side. When they did come to Norham, however, Edward promptly demanded that they acknowledge his suzerainty.

The Scots sought a delay to think about it and Edward reluctantly gave them three weeks to find an answer to his question—" Can you produce any evidence to show that I am not the rightful suzerain of Scotland? " At the end of May the Scots leaders delivered their answer, set out in courteous and conciliatory tone. They recapitulated Edward's undertaking to arbitrate in the matter of the rightful claimant to the throne, but as to the question of suzerainty they avoided direct conflict by claiming that they lacked the power to reply to the question " in the absence of the lord (the king of Scots) to whom such a demand should be addressed and who could reply to it." But they added, " the responsible men of the kingdom are willing that whoever shall be king shall perform to you whatever right and law require, for he and no one else will have the power to do this . . .".

Given the short time available to come up with a suitable reply the Scots did extremely well, but in effect they passed the buck to whoever should get the throne. Indeed, in the circumstances of a feudal society, they could do no other. The Scottish magnates could not answer on a matter which only the king could consider, and no decision of theirs could have been binding on any future king. Edward rejected this reply, but then approached the problem from another direction. He applied pressure on the would-be candidates and also the remaining Guardians on the grounds of expediency.

Scotland in the winter of 1290–1 and the early summer was in danger of disintegrating into civil war. Again, the Bruces were at the bottom of the trouble. A large body of magnates, including seven earls, rallied to the side of the Bruce. Towards the end of 1290 the earls of Angus, Atholl, Lennox, Mar, Menteith, Ross and Strathearn addressed a violent protest to the Guardians John Comyn and Bishop Fraser who had openly espoused the cause of John Balliol. The principal objection raised by the earls was that their ancient right of instituting the king had been swept aside by the Guardians, but this did not imply that they would refuse to recognize any decision taken by King Edward. Robert Bruce went so far as to seek Edward's recognition of the traditional law of succession and the rights of the seven earls in this matter. This petition, of course, dates from the autumn of 1290 when his position was much stronger than Balliol's and he was anxious merely to get Edward's endorsement. Later, however, he was much less inclined to abide by Edward's decision, when the case was going against him.

John Balliol was the younger son of the Lady Devorgilla and John Balliol of Barnard Castle in County Durham. Fortunately his brothers died in their father's lifetime and he gradually fell heir to vast estates in Durham and Northumberland as well as Galloway. Devorgilla's death in January 1290 brought Balliol to prominence in Scottish affairs. His position in County Durham gave him *entrée* to the influential Antony Bek, while his wife was the daughter of Earl Warenne, confidante and adviser of King Edward. History has dealt rather unkindly with John Balliol, attributing to him a certain fecklessness and lack of character, but even a much stronger personality than he might have fared no better in the tricky political situation of the 1290s.

Early in 1291 Edward instituted an exhaustive search in the religious houses for chronicles and other documentary evidence relating to Anglo-Scottish affairs, with a view to substantiating his claim to be the feudal superior of Scotland. There seems to have been some kind of rumour at the time that this search was intended as a prelude to the subjugation of Scotland but in fact it is highly unlikely that Edward had any such plan at that juncture, or indeed considered that such steps would be necessary.

On 10th May 1291 the Scottish leaders met King Edward and his advisers in the parish church of Norham on the Tweed about seven miles upstream from Berwick. According to the chronicler Hemingburgh a statement was drawn up by the Dominican provincial, William de Hotham, one of Edward's most trusted civil servants, and this was read to the Scots by Roger Brabazon. It set out the need for an acknowledgment by the claimants of Edward's superiority. There was some discussion about this the following day and then the meeting was adjourned till 2nd June. The resumption of talks coincided with the mustering of English forces in the northern counties on 3rd June at Norham, writs having been issued the previous April for this express purpose; the size of this force is not known but judging by the writs it must have been a substantial body.

There were nine meetings between 2nd and 13th June. Some were held on the village green of Upsettlington, on the Scottish bank of the Tweed, and others were held in Norham church, while two were convened in the king's apartments in the bishop's castle nearby. During this period the majority of the candidates, including both Balliol and Bruce, issued statements acknowledging Edward's superiority and agreeing to submit to his arbitration. They even went so far as to agree that Edward should take possession of the castles and other strongpoints of Scotland—despite the fact that none of the claimants had any power or authority to make such a concession. For his part Edward agreed to surrender these castles to the rightful king of Scots within two months of awarding the crown. Significantly he also promised that in future, on the death of a king, he would demand nothing but homage and the rights incidental to it.

This important admission was probably wrung from Edward by the efforts of Bishop Wishart who, all along, strenuously resisted Edward's claim and reiterated the words spoken by Alexander III in 1278. On 14th June, the day after the negotiations ended, Wishart and Bishop Crambeth of Dunkeld made independent copies of Edward's concession and annexed a document stating that the claimants' recognition of Edward's superiority had been made with the consent of the Guardians and the responsible men of the realm, thus indemnifying the claimants in case they had acted *ultra vires.*

On 11th June the Guardians resigned their authority and were immediately reappointed "by the most serene prince, the Lord Edward, by God's grace illustrious king of England, superior lord of Scotland". At the same time a fifth Guardian was appointed to secure Edward's interests, an English baron named Brian Fitz-Alan of Bedale.

Two days later, on the green of Upsettlington the Guardians and leading nobility of Scotland gathered to swear fealty to

Edward as superior and direct lord of the kingdom of Scotland. Among the notables present on that momentous occasion were Robert Bruce of Annandale and Robert Bruce, Earl of Carrick. Seven other earls of Scotland did homage that day and in the ensuing six weeks barons, knights, freemen and religious leaders personally swore fealty to Edward, who set the seal on his success by making a ceremonial progress through the kingdom. Finally, to save everyone else the trouble of doing homage in person, Ayr, Dumfries, Inverness and Perth were designated as centres for those who had not already done so. The deadline for taking the oath was 27th July—comparatively short notice —and severe penalties were to be imposed on those who refused or neglected to comply.

Although the submission of the Scots was far short of what Edward desired, it could not be said that they made much show of resisting his demands. The only sign of resistance was made by the Earl of Angus, Gilbert de Umfraville (an Englishman no less!) who refused to surrender Forfar and Dundee castles on the grounds that he had been appointed their custodian by the community of the realm of Scotland. This was merely a token show of resistance and the Guardians were not slow in finding a facesaving solution to this minor impasse.

Edward established a court of 104 auditors to decide who should have the crown and the preliminary hearing was fixed for 3rd August at Berwick. It has been suggested that Edward the lawyer took as his precedent the Roman *judicium centumvirile,* the court of 105 which settled questions of property in the time of the Roman republic. The court was composed of 24 auditors seconded from Edward's council, and 40 auditors nominated by Balliol and Bruce. Thus the claim of the other candidates was summarily dismissed and the court concentrated from the outset on the merits of the pleas put forward by the two principal protagonists. On 3rd August, however, all the competitors appeared at Berwick before Edward and the assembled auditors, formally to enter their petitions. These documents were sewn up in a sack secured with the seals of the earls of Buchan and Mar and the bishops of Glasgow and St. Andrews, and the sack then deposited in Berwick Castle. That done, Edward, who had pressing business elsewhere, adjourned the court until 2nd June of the following year. The court reassembled on 2nd June but was then adjourned once more until 14th October in order to allow the eighty Bruce and Balliol auditors time to consider their reply to the question by what laws and customs the right of succession should be determined. The actual hearings lasted from 14th October till 17th November when Edward gave judgment in favour of John Balliol. The eighty Scottish assessors were unable to agree about Scottish law and were unable to decide whether the rules of succession (which Edward had laid down for England in 1290) could or should also apply to Scotland. In the end they referred the matter back to Edward's council which decided, at the beginning of November, that primogeniture rather than nearness of issue should be the criterion and answered in favour of Balliol. The Scottish auditors were then asked to consider their verdict in the light of this decision and they, in turn, voted in favour of Balliol. Significantly Bishop Wishart, James the Steward and a few others declared that although they had originally favoured Bruce they had now been converted to Balliol by these legal arguments. On 6th November Edward gave judgment in favour of Balliol against Bruce and then turned to consider the claims of the other contestants against Balliol.

Having lost his claim to the throne of Scotland and believing that a third of a loaf is better than none at all, Bruce now lent his support to the claim of John Hastings of Abergavenny, grandson of Earl David's third daughter. Hastings argued that Scotland was not really a kingdom at all, that its kings were never crowned or annointed, and that it was no more than a big barony held of the king of England. As such it was partible between the descendants of David's three daughters—just as his earldoms of Chester and Northampton had been divided among Bruce and the fathers of Balliol and Hastings in 1237, following the death of John le Scot. Edward held, however, that Scotland was an impartible kingdom and dismissed the claim of Hastings.

On 17th November Roger Brabazon delivered the judgment in Edward's name. Two days later the constables of the 23 leading castles of the kingdom were ordered to surrender their charges to Balliol. The great seal of the Guardians was formally broken into four pieces and carefully stored away in the English treasury "lest, if the seal remained intact, doubts should arise about the authenticity of documents, and as a sign of the king of England's full sovereign lordship in the Scottish realm." On 20th November Balliol swore fealty to Edward at Norham, for the realm of Scotland held of him as superior lord. Ten days later, on St. Andrews' Day, John Balliol was installed on the stone at Scone by John de St. John deputizing for the infant Earl of Fife. At Newcastle on 26th December 1292, John Balliol did homage to his liege lord.

Chapter IV

The Reign of King John

During the interregnum of 1290–2 Robert of Annandale was involved in several rather shady operations. In the early part of 1290 he made an attempt to secure for himself the lordshire of Garioch in north-east Scotland. This district had belonged to Earl David and had been divided in 1237 between the Bruce, Balliol and Hastings descendants of the earl. Bruce did not feel that he himself could make a direct assault on the Balliol and Hastings rights to this lordship, so he made a contract with an influential friend, Sir Nicholas Biggar to bring an action in the Guardians' court against Balliol and Hastings by a royal brieve of right, to 'recover' for himself the lands held in Garioch by Balliol and Hastings. Just how such a claim was to be made has never been ascertained and on the face of it it seems difficult to see how the court could ever have upheld Biggar's claim. Bruce undertook to pay the costs of the case, while Biggar waived all his rights in the Garioch so that, had the action been successful, Bruce would have obtained sole rights in that area. In recompense for his trouble Biggar was to receive from Bruce forty merks worth of land south of the Forth for the token rent of a twentieth of a knight's service. This was no mere idle piece of land-grabbing, but a determined effort on Bruce's part to consolidate and increase his power in the north-east, linking the Garioch with the lands of two powerful Bruce supporters, the earls of Mar and Atholl.

To the spring of 1291 belongs the so-called Appeal of the Seven Earls, apparently addressed to Balliol and those of the Guardians who openly supported his claim. The opinion of past historians has been divided on the validity of this Appeal and, indeed, on the existence of the Seven Earls as an elective body. It now seems probable that the concept of the seven earls as electors was grounded in tradition and that, in the context of the thirteenth century, may have been enough to give their Appeal some weight. Quite clearly, however, the Appeal was Bruce's work, asserting as facts such dubious matters as his appointment by Alexander II as his tanist or heir in 1238, and his choice by the seven earls and the community of the realm. The Appeal, however, also contains a curious remark that, should the claims of Earl David's descendants be invalid, the rightful claimant would be Florence, Count of Holland.

As we have already seen, the Count's claim was a tenuous one, based on descent from Ada of Scotland, sister of William the Lion, but it hinged on the supposition that Earl David had resigned his rights to the Scottish throne (and therefore the rights of his descendants), in exchange for the lands of Garioch. Documents purporting to be copies of this resignation were prepared in November 1291 by the bishop of Moray and the Prior at Pluscarden and somehow or other the text of this resignation was used by Florence and his lawyers in the debate over his claim in November 1292, though he asserted, at the time, that the document had been detained by the Prior of Pluscarden and was not available for examination.

This is one of those mysteries which have still to be unravelled. Did the two prelates copy the document in good faith, or did they perpetrate a deliberate forgery? In withholding the precious copy was the prior acting for, or against Count Florence? And what was Bruce's part in this? The latter question can be answered. On 14th June 1292 Bruce entered into an agreement with Florence, whereby if either of them were successful he should enfeoff the other with a third part of the kingdom. The successful claimant was also to have first option of taking a lease of this third if the other should wish to let it for rent. Furthermore, if Bruce were successful he was to grant Florence his English estates to the value of one third of the royal demesne of Scotland—but no such proviso was made in the event of Florence being successful. Sir Maurice Powicke argues that this indenture proved that Bruce regarded the Dutchman as his most formidable rival, but the one-sidedness of the agreement denies this. Undoubtedly Bruce continued to regard Balliol as his only serious opponent and involved Florence only on the grounds that anything was worth trying if it might help defeat Balliol. Bruce assumed that if Florence's claim were valid it would only serve to eliminate Balliol's only claim (on descent from Earl David). It would also eliminate Bruce's rather weaker claim on the same ground, but would not invalidate his other claims to the throne, based on tanistry and the dictum that might is right.

The elimination of Bruce in favour of Balliol on 6th November 1292 was not the end of the matter so far as Bruce was concerned. The following day he drew up a document delegating his claim to the throne to his son, the Earl of Carrick, and his heirs. This impressive document, now in the British Museum, was sealed by Bruce and Gilbert de Clare, Earl of Gloucester. Two days later, on 9th November, the Earl of Carrick resigned his earldom to his son, the eighteen year-old Robert. The Countess Marjorie had died earlier in the year and it was in the natural order of things for her eldest son to succeed to the title. In August 1293 the young earl was confirmed in the succession at the parliament convened at Stirling, James the Steward and the Earl of Mar acting as his sponsors. The elder Earl of Carrick, having divested himself of his responsibilities in Ayrshire, left Scotland to travel in Europe and studiously avoided having to do homage for his lands to a king whom he despised. In 1293 he was in Norway for the marriage of his daughter Isabel to Eirik II. This marriage resumed Norwegian interest in Scottish affairs. For the moment, however, it was a match with which Edward I was well satisfied, since the Bruces were at that time on good terms with the English court. Moreover, the Competitor, having resigned his claim, had faded out of the political picture. He retired to his castle of Lochmaben in the heart of his Annandale estates where he died in 1295 in his eighty-fifth year.

Right from the beginning of the new reign Edward made it clear that his superiority was to continue. Before the year was out Edward demonstrated at least one aspect of this by deciding a case at Newcastle, an appeal by a burgess of Berwick against the action of the justiciars and assessors whom Edward had appointed to deal with Scottish cases after the kingdom had

(*right*) The cave at Cove, near Kirkpatrick Fleming, Dumfriesshire, traditional site of Bruce's legendary incident with the spider. The cave is half-way up a sheer cliff, fifty feet above the River Annan. (*below*) The Pass of Brander, Argyll

(*above left*) The statue of Bruce at Stirling Castle; (*above right*) The Bruce Memorial at Bannockburn; (*below*) General view of the battlefield: the Bannock Burn is in the foreground, while the flagstaff marks the site of Bruce's headquarters during the battle

been entrusted to him. When the Scots protested at this, as a clear violation of the Treaty of Birgham-Northampton which had ensured the right of Scots to plead or answer for offences only in their own country, Edward clarified the position, first through Roger Brabazon and then in a personal statement to King John, the prelates and magnates of Scotland and England assembled at Newcastle for the Christmas feast.

John Balliol's position was weakened inevitably when, on 2nd January 1293, he formally undertook to respect the validity of the acts done by Edward as lord while the kingdom was in his trust, in order to maintain the continuity of justice and government. Inevitably also, closer ties between Scotland and England, stretching back over at least two generations, created the right atmosphere for the events of 1293–6. During that period Edward kept up social and legal contacts with influential figures in Scotland, at all levels of society, and this insidiously undermined the independence and authority of John Balliol. It was not surprising therefore that the mayor and burgesses of the Scottish town of Berwick could describe Edward, in a petition of 1294, as ruling the three realms of England, Scotland and Ireland by divine providence. Gradually a practice arose of appealing from the Scottish to the English courts. In 1293 alone Edward heard appeals from the court of King John, raised by John le Mazun or Mason of Bordeaux and Macduff of Fife, son of a previous earl, who claimed lands in Fife. When Balliol or his representatives failed to appear in the English court to defend his actions, Edward and his lawyers devised a code of regulations, based on common law procedure, aimed at controlling and penalizing John's disobedience. Edward might well have argued that he was solely concerned with the maintenance of law and order in the northern realm, and he did not deliberately go out of his way to undermine John's position. There was a head-on clash between Edward and his vassal in the Michaelmas session of parliament at Westminster when John appeared at last to answer in the case of Macduff. John refused to answer or even to seek an adjournment (since that would have admitted recognition of the court). Balliol backed down and begged, as Edward's man for the realm of Scotland, for a day to take counsel. He promised to give an answer in the next parliament. This issue was never resolved. The wars in

Wales and France intervened and by 1295 the situation had deteriorated beyond the point of retrieval.

In October 1293, however, Edward got a taste of his own medicine. As Duke of Aquitaine he was a vassal of the king of France and Philip summoned him to answer for the crimes of some English seamen who had gone on the rampage in the port of La Rochelle. Although he avoided a personal appearance Edward was forced to send his representatives to Philip's court, to submit and make formal surrender of his French fiefs on 5th March 1294. Smarting under this humiliation, Edward formed an alliance with his sons-in-law, the Duke of Brabant and the Count of Bar, and the rulers of Franche Comte and the Low Countries and declared war on his liege lord in October 1294. Philip neutralized the Emperor Adolf, won over Count Florence the late contender for the Scottish throne, and made a treaty of friendship with Eirik II. The situation looked grim for Edward, who also had a rebellion in Wales to deal with, and he ordered the king of Scotland to muster his forces and assemble at London by 1st September 1294. John received this summons at the end of June and within a few days tooks steps to defy his master. A parliament was convened at Stirling in July and twelve advisers were appointed to assist the king—four representatives of the earls, the barons and the bishops. Bishops Fraser of St. Andrews and Crambeth of Dunkeld, together with two of the barons, formed an embassy despatched to the French court to arrange a marriage between Edward Balliol, the king's son and heir, and Jeanne de Valois, Philip's niece. On 22nd October 1295 the treaties with Norway and Scotland were approved and made public in Paris and the impending marriage contract celebrated. Eirik II, in consideration of an annual payment of some £50,000 sterling, undertook to supply a battle fleet of a hundred ships for four months each year as long as hostilities between England and France continued. King John undertook, for his part, to invade England if Edward left the country or sent forces across the Channel to make war on France. In return Philip promised support to Scotland.

During the summer of 1295 Edward was all too well aware of the secret Franco-Scottish negotiations and early in October he prepared to secure his northern defences against possible attack. On 5th October he appointed Antony Bek and Balliol's father-in-law, Earl Warenne, custodians of the northern shires. Warenne was also appointed governor of Bamborough Castle and Robert Bruce, formerly Earl of Carrick and now lord of Annandale, as governor of Carlisle Castle. He ordered Balliol to surrender the castles and burghs of Berwick, Jedburgh and Roxburgh. Finally, on 16th October, he issued writs to all the sheriffs in England for the seizure of the English estates, goods and chattels of King John. Two months later he summoned more than 200 of his tenants to muster at Newcastle in March 1296 fully armed and equipped. In February 1296 he assembled a fleet of ships in East Anglia and proceeded up the east coast, to rendezvous with his land forces at Newcastle. John retaliated by issuing a national call to arms for 11th March, summoning all free men to Caddonlee four miles north of Selkirk.

The Bruces were conspicuous by their absence from this muster. Since the accession of King John the Bruce family, by and large, had lain low. The elder Earl of Carrick had expressed himself forcibly by resigning his earldom to avoid homage to Balliol. The marriage of his daughter Isabel to Eirik of Norway was sanctioned by Edward and seemed likely at first to cause embarrassment to the Scottish government; it was certainly a matter much debated by Balliol's council of twelve, who were uncertain of the loyalty of the Bruce faction to the country. In 1294 The Competitor wangled the election of his own nominee, Thomas Dalton of Kirkcudbright as Bishop of Galloway. Episcopal appointments were theoretically in the king's gift and John Balliol had opposed this election. Furthermore the diocese of Galloway was co-terminous with Balliol's own estates, yet the neighbouring landowner of Annandale had had the effrontery to challenge him in this way. The clergy of the diocese were split down the middle between Balliol and Bruce and it was alleged that the Bruces had bribed the prior and canons of Whithorn whose privilege it was to elect the bishop. Dalton is a small village some five miles south of Lochmaben and it is presumed that Master Thomas had close family ties with Annandale. And now the appointment of the new lord of Annandale as governor of Carlisle indicated where the Bruce sympathies lay, in the event of a confrontation between Edward and Balliol.

A number of Scottish magnates, including the Bruces, ignored Balliol's summons and were promptly dispossessed. Annandale was assigned to the Earl of Buchan, and the Earls of Angus and Dunbar were similarly ejected from their lands for siding with Edward. The young Earl of Carrick and his brother Nigel were with their father in Carlisle in March 1296 when war actually broke out.

The first skirmish in the hostilities was a curious, half-cock affair. Robert de Ros, lord of Wark and an Englishman, was in love with a Scots girl whom he wished to marry. He deserted to the Scottish side and late in March led a party of Scots from Roxburgh on an attack on Wark castle. The attack fizzled out and the Scots failed to take this strongpoint. Edward moved north and raised the siege of Wark, where he was met by the Bruces on 25th March and received homage from them for their lands in Scotland. Three days later the English army crossed the Tweed and on 30th March invested the town of Berwick. The attack on Berwick began inauspiciously. Four of the English ships taking part in combined operations ran aground in the mouth of the river; the townspeople counter-attacked by the sea gate, burned the ships and killed or captured their crews. Apart from this initial success the town was doomed. The richest commercial centre in Scotland was poorly defended by earthworks surmounted by a wooden stockade. Edward attacked in force from the landward side and his shock troops swept over the palisade at the first assault. Later the Scots put out a story of English cunning, of cavalry flying false colours tricking the defenders into opening the gates, but the truth was more prosaic. The English overran the ramparts throwing the townsmen into confusion. Virtually the only resistance was put up by the small Flemish colony who held the Red Hall until they were engulfed in the fire which razed it to the ground.

Quarter was given to the castle garrison, commanded by Sir William Douglas known as le Hardi, whom Edward retained as a hostage. In contrast, however, Edward did not spare the town itself. Edward had attempted to parley with the burgesses of Berwick but they had taunted him with obscene doggerel and rude gestures. His revenge was thorough, even by the standards of the time. Thousands of men, women and children were put to the sword, their houses looted and burned. The sack of

Berwick in 1296 was meant to be a lesson to the rebellious Scots; it sparked off a bitterness which took centuries to eradicate. The death toll published in various contemporary chronicles varied from a maximum of 60,000 (Matthew of Westminster) to a minimum of 7,000 quoted by the Scottish historian John of Fordoun a generation later. Allowing for the fact that a body count was something to be proud of in medieval terms (and, conversely, Fordoun would be anxious to minimize the "success" of the English) it can be assumed that the true figure was somewhere between these estimates. This atrocity was heightened by the fact that it had been committed by a people supposedly friendly to the Scots for generations, after the briefest of assaults in which English casualties had been remarkably light. The raping and murder continued despite the pleading of the clergy for clemency. Edward rode around the town viewing the carnage with satisfaction, and it was only the gruesome spectacle of a woman in childbirth being felled by a sword which moved him to call off the slaughter.

The Scots had not been inactive. On Easter Monday a large army of foot soldiers led by John of Badenoch and seven earls of Scotland (including Atholl, Ross and Menteith) forded the Solway and marched on Carlisle burning villages and hamlets en route. They did considerable damage to the houses on the outskirts of the town but they were unable to overcome the walled defences. Under the able command of the lord of Annandale and the young Earl of Carrick the townspeople beat off the Scots attack. The Scots withdrew on 28th March and recrossed the Solway into Annandale, leaving its erstwhile lord in command of Cumberland. When news of the sack of Berwick reached the Scottish army the earls despatched punitive expeditions across the Cheviot Hills, raiding and burning at will throughout the dales of Northumberland. Much of the ensuing destruction was aimless and seems to have been in the nature of reprisals for the Berwick atrocities. A propaganda document, supposedly prepared for dissemination in France to show King Philip what savages he was allied to, states of the Scots: "They burned about 200 little scholars who were in the school at Corbridge learning their first letters and grammar, having blocked up the doors and set fire to the building." The Lanercost Chronicle, however, given a different location for this atrocity, stating " They collected a crowd of young schoolboys in Hexham school and, blocking the doors, set fire to the building and its inmates innocent in the sight of God." Walter of Guisborough mentions the burning of Hexham and its priory but makes no mention of the murder of the schoolboys.

In fact the Scottish raids in Redesdale and Tynedale served little purpose, and did not deflect Edward from his grand designs for the subjugation of Scotland. Berwick was to be the pivot on which the administration of Scotland was the balance, and with characteristic energy Edward set to work as early as April to rebuild the town so recently sacked by his troops. He recruited a vast work force in Northumberland and personally supervised the initial stages at least of the town's reconstruction. The ineffectual earthworks were replaced by a deep ditch and high, broad earthworks. Having secured the defences Edward then designated, in September 1296, Berwick as the administrative centre for the government of Scotland and appointed Hugh Cressingham, formerly chief itinerant justice for the northern counties of England, as Treasurer of Scotland with his headquarters in the town. In January 1297 a committee was established to advise on the planning of the new town under the direction of Cressingham.

Almost a month elapsed after the fall of Berwick before Edward resumed the offensive. No doubt he realized that time was on his side, and that the pacification of Scotland would be a relatively simple matter. The king of Scots had already been shown up as weak and ineffective—" a lamb among wolves " is how one chronicler was to describe him. The magnates of Scotland were divided, ranging from those, like the Bruces, who were actively engaged on Edward's behalf, to the Earl of Buchan, Constable of Scotland, who was attempting to co-ordinate Scottish resistance to Edward. In between were earls and barons who could not decide where their interests lay, or who would not serve under leaders with whom they disagreed.

On 23rd April the main English army commanded by Balliol's father-in-law, Earl Warenne, set out along the coast road from Berwick north into the Lothians and four days later engaged the Scots under Buchan at Dunbar. The earls of Mar and Atholl, traditional supporters of the Bruce faction, decided at the last moment not to take part in the battle and the loss of their troops to the Scottish side was a sad blow to Buchan. Like the Scots of 1651 before Cromwell, Buchan's army lost what little advantage they had by rushing headlong from the high ground to charge the English cavalry. The struggle was unequal and Buchan's army was destroyed. With this signal defeat resistance in Scotland crumpled completely. Among those taken prisoner at Dunbar were the earls of Atholl, Ross and Menteith, the son of John Comyn of Badenoch and half a dozen other magnates and they were speedily transported south, to be incarcerated in various English castles. The Steward surrendered Roxburgh Castle, Edinburgh Castle was battered by English siege engines and the Lowlands easily subdued. By the middle of June Edward was at Stirling, where an Irish contingent led by Richard de Burgh joined him. From there the English army proceeded in a leisurely fashion northwards through Perth, Montrose, Aberdeen and Banff as far as Elgin. Detachments were sent westward into the Highlands but the main body moved south again at the end of July. On 2nd July John Balliol, from his temporary headquarters at Kincardine, formally confessed his error in making an alliance with France against his liege lord and surrendered his kingdom to Edward. The letter which he sent to Edward bore the great seal of Scotland, probably the last time he sealed documents with this device. Five days later, in the churchyard of Stracathro, Balliol publicly admitted his errors and confirmed his reconciliation with Edward. On 10th July he underwent two humiliating ceremonies; at Brechin he formally surrendered his enfeoffment to Antony Bek, and later the same day he repeated it to Edward himself at Montrose. His act of submission was total. Edward, with a fine sense of the dramatic, had the royal insignia ceremonially ripped from Balliol's tabard or surcoat, and from this humiliating incident springs the nickname by which the luckless Balliol has ever since been known—Toom Tabard (empty coat). Later generations have confused this nickname, taking it to mean that he was a hollow king, a mere puppet manipulated by Edward, and this harsh though erroneous concept is repeated forcibly by Agnes Mure Mackenzie, maintaining that the quality of his reign made his subjects call him "Empty Jacket". In another age and in other circumstances John Balliol might have shown more positive and statesmanlike qualities. His principal misfortune was to take over a divided country which had been without a leader for six years, and to be faced with the ruthless opportunism of a powerful neighbour.

Early in August John Balliol and his son Edward were taken by sea to England under the escort of Thomas of Lancaster. For a brief spell he was kept in the Tower of London but shortly thereafter he was allowed a measure of liberty—the modern equivalent would be house arrest—at Hertford not far from his former manor of Hitchin. He was given every comfort in accordance with a man of his position, including a huntsman and ten hounds. When the revolt of Wallace, Comyn and Moray broke out in 1297 in the name of King John, he and his son were returned to the Tower. Two years later the Balliols, father and son, were handed over to the papal legate with whom they sojourned for a while. In 1302 John Balliol was released from this amiable custody and allowed to retire to his estate at Bailleul in Picardy where he died in 1314, the year of Bannockburn. His son Edward was to return to Scotland in 1333 and reigned for five years as a puppet backed up by the forces of Edward III, but thereafter he faded from the scene and died, at an advanced age, in 1370.

The inherent weakneses of Scotland, together with the character defects and vacillation of John Balliol, make this reign one of the most tragic in a history noted for tragedy. The submissions at Stracathro, Brechin and Montrose which brought this sorry reign to an end plunged Scotland into a decade in which the national identity was all but obliterated.

CHAPTER V

William Wallace

HENCEFORWARD Scotland was merely an extension of England. To signify this Edward removed the ancient Stone of Destiny from Scone, where the kings of Scotland had been installed for centuries. The great seal was broken up and three large chests of royal records removed from Edinburgh. The Scottish regalia, including the Black Rood of St. Margaret, was also transferred to England.

According to an anonymous account, Edward held his parliament at Berwick on 28th August 1296.

> And there were all the bishops, earls, barons, abbots and priors; and there he received the homage of all, and their oaths that they would be good and loyal to him. To the well regulated people he forthwith gave up all their own goods and those of their tenants; the earls, barons and bishops he permitted to enjoy their lands, provided they came at All Saints to the parliament at St Edmunds. Then he appointed the Earl Warenne to be guardian of the land, and sir Hugh de Cressingham treasurer, sir Walter of Amersham chancellor. Then he tarried at Berwick three weeks and three days, arranging his affairs, and set out on his road to England on the Sunday after the feast of the Holy Cross.

The main business of the Berwick parliament was the assembly of more than two thousand Scottish landowners, clergy, burgesses and representatives of communities to do homage to Edward, not as superior of Scotland but as King of England, Lord of Ireland and Duke of Guyenne. Geoffrey Barrow is sceptical about the size of this assembly, which it would have been impracticable to handle, far less take each person through the prescribed ritual in turn. He is of the opinion that certain limited and well-defined classes of persons who held property in Scotland were required to provide written and sealed instruments of homage and fealty. The bulk of the names on the so-called Ragman Roll consisted of tenants-in-chief of the Crown and their heirs, substantial subtenants and their heirs, officers and leading burgesses of some eastern burghs, heads of religious houses and other clergy. The names were collected in order of sheriffdoms and for this reason certain people, with extensive holdings in several shires, appear on the Roll more than once.

Among the names were those of Robert Bruce lord of Annandale and his son the Earl of Carrick, who had already sworn fealty to Edward the previous March. It is said by Fordoun that the elder Bruce reminded Edward of a promise, made when Balliol first showed signs of revolt, that the Scottish throne would be assigned to him. To this Edward replied testily "Have we nothing else to do but win you kingdoms?" If the elder Bruce made any reply to this it has gone unrecorded. At any rate he returned to his duties at Carlisle without demur. From Edward's viewpoint it is understandable that having just toppled one figurehead in Scotland he was not going to establish another. History has an impression of the elder Bruce as a somewhat colourless, spineless individual—not unlike John Balliol, in fact—but Edward knew him personally and may have feared that Scotland would not be so easily handled under his rule. As for the young Earl of Carrick, those qualities of character—ambition, determination and resolution—which won him the throne would already be well-formed. In the autumn of 1296 the Earl of Carrick was turned twenty-two, a well set-up young man with a mind of his own.

On the other hand, if he perceived the wisdom of not handing over Scotland to the Bruces Edward undeniably erred in establishing in Scotland a form of government so totally subordinate to England. He might easily have appointed yet another body of Guardians, and there were sufficient Scotsmen of good will, anxious to serve him, whom he could have appointed his officers for the administration of the government at every level. The status of Scotland was kept deliberately vague. The kingdom was not abolished but merely kept in suspension and Edward did not add any Scottish title to his name.

Although the Earl Warenne was Edward's Keeper (or lieutenant) in Scotland he took little or no interest in Scottish affairs and preferred to reside in Yorkshire. The actual day to day business of administering the conquered kingdom was left to a body of low-born officials—John Benstead, John Droxford, Ralph Manton, William Ormsby, John Sandal, Philip Willoughby and others. These men administered Scotland efficiently in the interests of their master, though the means by which they achieved this might often be seen by the Scots as high-handed, unjust and corrupt.

In the midst of all this turmoil and commotion the Earl of Carrick was stricken by bereavement. In 1294 he married Isabel, daughter of Donald Earl of Mar. In 1296 she bore him a daughter, named Marjorie after his mother. Isabel died soon after this. At the same time the Bruce estates in Scotland, which Balliol had taken from them in October 1295 and assigned to the Earl of Buchan, were restored to the lord of Annandale and his son. While the elder Bruce continued to serve as Governor of Carlisle Castle, the Earl of Carrick attended to the problems of restoring order to the family estates. Rents were in arrears and there were many domestic matters to be sorted out. He had considerable debts outstanding to the Exchequer; Edward granted him a postponement till his affairs were in order.

Edward returned to England late in 1296 well pleased with himself. He had subdued Scotland, established a system for its good government, and eliminated a potential thorn in his side. He could now concentrate his attention on the impending campaign with France. The natural leaders of Scotland, the earls and barons, were either prisoners in England or by their past conduct had demonstrated their loyalty to Edward. The policy of harnessing Scotland to England seemed to be a natural one which would progress smoothly. There is no doubt, however, that Edward misjudged the situation and his over-confidence blinded him to the ominous signs of future trouble. There was a certain amount of passive resistance among the clergy; only three out of the twelve bishops, for example, subscribed to Ragman Roll. Three bishops, including Fraser of St. Andrews, a staunch Balliol supporter, chose to absent themselves from the country and others, like the bishop of Argyll and the bishop of Sodor and Man, were too remote from the centre of things to care much anyway. Though the nobility and gentry had shown more positive support for Edward and his policy there were some significant absentees from the Roll. The section pertaining to the Steward's lands in Renfrew and Paisley is comparatively detailed and lists many lesser tenants. Conspicuous by their absence were the names of Malcolm and William Wallace who held land of the Steward in Elderslie near Paisley. It seems probable that the sheriff of Lanark failed to secure the homages of these brothers because they chose deliberately to flout the command. This may explain the references by Walter of Guisborough in his chronicle to William Wallace as an outlaw prior to the commencement of the revolt in 1297.

The revolt of 1297 was no carefully planned or co-ordinated rising. It seems to have started with sporadic outbreaks of anti-English violence in the more remote parts of the country, in the Highlands and in Galloway. In May came the celebrated incident involving young William Wallace at Lanark in which he slew the unpopular English sheriff Heselrig. With a small band of followers he moved westward to Ayr; by midsummer the whole south-west of Scotland was aflame with revolt. Although discontent with English rule gave the rising its spontaneous character it would not have succeeded as far as it did without the support of certain influential men. Chief among these were James the Steward and Bishop Wishart of Glasgow, the two surviving Guardians of 1286. Wishart had many kinsmen well placed in the church, and the medieval church was admirably suited to subversive activities, providing the organization and the communication whereby the revolt was maintained. Sir William Douglas, late governor of Berwick Castle, had been released from confinement late in 1296 and lost no time in aligning himself with the rebels. Edward ordered the Earl of Carrick to muster the men of Annandale and launch an attack on the Douglas stronghold. According to the Guisborough chronicler the bishop of Carlisle suspected the loyalty of young Bruce and made him swear a special oath of allegiance to Edward before setting out on the expedition, but this may be no more than a fiction of hindsight.

Bruce and his forces marched over the hills from Dumfriesshire and down the valley of the Clyde to Douglasdale whose castle was being held by Sir William's English wife, Eleanor Ferrers. She was his second wife, a widow whom he had forcibly abducted while visiting Scotland, but she was completely loyal to the Scottish cause. Sir William himself had gone to Ayr to join the main body of rebels. The Earl of Carrick made no more than a token attack on Douglas Castle, but then abruptly, and for no apparent reason, changed sides. Walter of Guisborough explains this *volte face* simply by saying that Bruce joined the Scots because he was a Scotsman. Young Robert addressed his father's tenants of Annandale before the walls of Douglas Castle, "No man holds his own flesh and blood in hatred and I am no exception. I must join my own people and the nation in which I was born." He said that his oath at Carlisle had been given under duress and he appealed to the Annandale men to join him but with the exception of a few they apparently declined. Their loyalty was to the earl's father and he was Edward's governor at Carlisle. The Annandale levies slipped back over the hills to Dumfriesshire while the young earl and his supporters, with the men of Douglasdale and Lady Douglas and her family, journeyed westward into Ayrshire. In Carrick he had no trouble in recruiting his own tenants.

The action of the Earl of Carrick at Douglas was his crossing of the Rubicon. He had a strong position in Scotland and was almost a protégé of Edward. Why give all that up for some vague concept of Scottishness which barely existed? Wishart and the Steward were life-long supporters of the Bruce faction, but Sir William Douglas was a staunch Balliol man—and the uprising was nominally on Balliol's behalf. Why go against family interest in support of the traditional rival of his house? It has been said that as early as 1297 the Earl of Carrick had aspirations to the throne, but this is highly unlikely and there is nothing, in the events during the revolt from 1297 to 1304 to suggest this.

Andrew de Moray raised his standard at Avoch in the Black Isle and harried the English garrisons in the north-east. William Wallace employed the same guerrilla tactics in the south-west and raided Scone, held by justiciar Ormsby, and Glasgow where Antony Bek was then in residence. Elsewhere, however, the revolt was something of a damp squib. Edward, at this time pre-occupied with his Continental campaign, could not come north to sort out the rebellious Scots himself, but he delegated the task to Earl Warenne and he called out the northern English shires. His grandson, Henry Percy, and Robert Clifford, influential men in Northumberland and Westmorland respectively, commanded the English levies which marched through Annandale, up the Nith valley and down by Cumnock into Ayrshire towards the end of June. They came up with the Scots army at Irvine north of Ayr. The Scottish leaders took one look at Percy's heavy cavalry and decided to throw in the towel. Disunion among the leaders demoralized the rank and file. Sir Richard Lundin, disgusted at the vacillation of the commanders, promptly went over to the English side.

The Steward, showing some of that wile for which his Stewart descendants were later to be renowned, managed to spin out the surrender negotiations for several weeks, gaining valuable time for Wallace and Moray whose hit-and-run tactics were beginning to pay off. Indeed, Wishart, Bruce and the Steward managed to use the surrender negotiations as a political platform. The bishop, the baron and the earl began to talk as if they were Guardians anew. Some time before the end of July, however, Wishart and Sir William Douglas were captured by the English and the Steward was only permitted to go free on giving substantial sureties for his good behaviour. But the negotiations regarding the Earl of Carrick were protracted till the end of the year. He was asked to hand over his little daughter Marjorie as a guarantee of his good behaviour but he cavilled at this and continued to delay matters, evading the issue of coming in to the king's peace.

By the end of the year the English administration in Scotland was virtually bankrupt. Treasurer Cressingham was having the greatest difficulty in raising revenue and his officials had been roughly handled; the widespread campaign of civil disobedience had gone from a passive to an active role and in some counties the Scots had re-established their own bailiffs and officials, contemptuously ignoring the English system. A similar situation developed in southern Ireland in 1919–21. And all this time Wallace and Andrew de Moray continued their run of military successes and had mobilized considerable forces, mainly of infantry drawn from the commonalty of Scotland. Undoubtedly

Moray and Wallace received the overt assistance of the Scottish magnates though their part in this campaign is more shadowy, and the church certainly helped to co-ordinate the resistance. Late in August the forces of Wallace and Moray were joined; the men of north and south converged on Stirling, whither the English army led by Earl Warenne and Cressingham was bound for a grand showdown. The Scots took up defensive positions on the southern slope of the Abbey Craig, a mile north of the narrow bridge spanning the river Forth. It was a well-chosen position. From the bridge ran a causeway across marsh and soft ground impassable to heavy mail-clad destriers, and beyond, on either flank, the river looped and meandered across the plain. Wallace's plan seems to have been simply to lure Warenne across the bridge and the causeway and to encircle his men as they struggled up the Abbey Craig out of the plain. This was the situation at the beginning of September when the Scots and English confronted each other across the Forth.

A number of Scottish magnates, including the Steward and the Earl of Lennox, visited the English camp and promised to parley with the Scots to prevent unnecessary bloodshed. They returned on 10th September, their mission unfulfilled, but then promised instead to contribute a squadron of cavalry to the English army. A slight skirmish with some English soldiers, one of whom was killed, seemed to belie the validity of this promise. It is more than likely that Lennox and the Steward were merely spying out the land for their compatriots and had no intention of taking part on the English side.

The action on 11th September had the typically farcical elements of many a military manoeuvre before and since. A strong force of infantry was sent across the bridge at dawn—but recalled because Earl Warenne was still asleep. When the commander eventually rose the infantrymen were sent across the bridge a second time—but again they were recalled when Lennox and the Steward staged an appearance. Warenne, no doubt hoping that the Scots wished to surrender as they had done at Irvine, decided to keep " a low profile " and cool the situation while negotiations proceeded. But the Scottish emissaries brought no plea of surrender, only the abject excuse that they had failed to win over any of their men from Wallace's ranks.

Next Warenne (who seems to have been most reluctant to commit his forces to battle) sought the intercession of the church, Two Dominicans were despatched to the Scottish lines to see if Wallace would submit. Instead he replied, "Tell your commander that we are not here to make peace but to do battle to defend ourselves and liberate our kingdom. Let them come on, and we shall prove this in their very beards." Sir Richard Lundin, the very knight who had deserted in disgust at Irvine, suggested to Warenne that the river was easily fordable some way upstream and that a sizeable force could get across and outflank the Scots. But the English army had delayed long enough. Lundin's sound advice was ignored and Warenne, urged on by Cressingham, ordered his troops across the narrow bridge, where only two knights could pass side by side. It says a great deal for the disciplinary powers of Moray and Wallace that the Scots held firm until a considerable party of English cavalry had crossed the bridge and deployed themselves on the poor ground on either side of the causeway. It also says much for Wallace's sense of timing; at the right moment he sent his spearmen headlong down the slope and through the water meadows to cut the English in two at the bridge. The English north of the bridge found themselves unable to manoeuvre and those south of the bridge were unable to reinforce them. The English advance party was trapped in a loop of the river, twenty feet deep with a rising spring tide and a dangerously fast current. Some Welsh archers, lightly clad, succeeded in swimming across the river to safety and a few cavalry led by Sir Marmaduke Tweng (a distant kinsman of the Bruces) hacked their way back over the bridge before the Scots cut loose its timbers. But the flower of the English knighthood was slaughtered and a great many infantry besides, while Warenne watched helplessly from the southern bank and his men panicked into a disorderly rout. Some accounts state that Warenne himself gave the order for the bridge to be destroyed, to prevent the Scots following up their success. He placed Stirling Castle in the care of Tweng and Sir William Fitz Warin and then took off as fast as his horse and his advanced years would allow, not pausing to draw breath or fodder his beast until he was safely within the walls of Berwick. "And", adds one account, "that horse never was able to eat corn again."

The treasurer Cressingham perished on the field of battle that day, skewered by the Scottish spearmen. Afterwards they skinned his corpse and cut up his pelt into little pieces which people carried all over Scotland as a kind of talisman, a symbol of release from the hated regime which Cressingham had represented.

Though Earl Warenne got away to safety his army fared less well. The Steward and Lennox, whose part in recent events had been strange to say the least, seized the opportunity to ambush the retreating English in the marshlands of the Forth known as the Pows and capture vast quantities of baggage and equipment.

In terms of men and material the Battle of Stirling Bridge was a small affair, but in the context of the struggle for independence its importance was immeasurable. A highly trained and equipped army had been defeated by a much smaller band of irregulars. English knights had been brought low by an infantry force largely composed of the peasants and lower classes. The Scots army at Dunbar had been an ill-disciplined rabble; at Irvine its behaviour had been ludicrous. Now the Scots were showing a new determination to stand their ground and fight "to defend ourselves and liberate our kingdom". Given the right leader the Scots could prove to the world at large that they were the equal of one of the finest fighting forces in medieval Europe.

Overnight Wallace became *de facto* ruler of Scotland—or at least those growing areas liberated from English administration. Within a month he and Moray were dealing, in the name of the community of the realm, with the powerful Hanseatic League. It was a case of "business as usual"; trade between Scotland and northern Europe was being restored despite the loss of Berwick. Moray died in November, supposedly of wounds sustained at Stirling Bridge, and thenceforward Wallace was sole ruler of Scotland, styling himself "William Wallace, knight, Guardian of the kingdom of Scotland and commander of its armies, in the name of the famous prince the lord John, by God's grace illustrious king of Scotland, by consent of the community of that realm."

England in the latter part of 1297 was in a parlous state. Edward was compaigning in France, but back at home political and financial crises were looming large. Edward's two principal lieutenants, the Constable Hereford and the Earl Marshal Norfolk, openly defied the king and denounced their fealty. The church refused to pay the tax levied by Edward for the prosecution of his foreign wars—half a year's income—and also repudiated its corporate fealty. Edward was in no position to do much about Scotland, though certain measures were taken which indicate the situation. Orders were given for the replacement of the Scots prelates by Englishmen—evidence of the complicity of the Scottish clergy in the resistance movement. In October the lord of Annandale was dismissed from his post as governor of Carlisle Castle and superseded by the local bishop. The Bishop of Carlisle subsequently received orders from Westminster promulgated on 14th November, to prepare to receive the Earl of Carrick into the King's peace, but there is no evidence that the younger Bruce complied with this, and, in the circumstances, it would be exceedingly unlikely that he did.

During the months of October and November 1297 Wallace took the offensive, staging a large-scale invasion of Northumbria which had little military value but demonstrated by its severity that the Scots meant business. Using Rothbury Forest as their base war parties roamed at will, looting, killing, raping and burning wherever they went. The systematic terrorization of the northern shires was so thorough that refugees fled from towns and villages as far south as County Durham at the mere thought of the Scots coming. The discipline which had marked the Scottish ranks at Stirling was now singularly lacking. In formal engagements the Scots fared poorly and failed to capture any of the towns, from Berwick to Durham and Carlisle, to which they laid siege. A severe winter set in early that year and it was General Frost who eventually defeated the Scots, driving them back over the Cheviots at the end of November. In Scotland the beleaguered English garrisons in Edinburgh and Roxburgh held out, but Stirling Castle capitulated through hunger. Wallace spared the lives of its commanders, who included William de Ros, brother of the turncoat Robert de Ros of Wark.

In November, while campaigning in northern England, Wallace secured the election of Master William Lamberton as Bishop of St. Andrews in place of Bishop Fraser who had recently died at Auteuil in France. Lamberton, whose family hailed from Berwickshire, was the chancellor of Glasgow cathedral and an avowed patriot. The political implications of this appointment amounted to a further act of defiance against Edward and the strengthening of the patriotic faction among the higher clergy of Scotland. Lamberton subsequently travelled to Rome to have his appointment confirmed by Pope Boniface. Lamberton was absent on the Continent for almost two years, combining his pilgrimage to the Holy See with a diplomatic mission which resulted in the release of John Balliol from English custody into the hands of the Papal Legate. Boniface VIII also wrote on several occasions to Edward urging him to desist in his attacks on Scotland and, finally, declaring that Scotland was subject to the Papacy and demanding that the dispute between Edward and the Scots should be brought before the Pope for judgment. Lamberton failed to persuade Philip of France to send an expeditionary force to Scotland under Charles of Valois, though the French king continued to give his moral and diplomatic support to Scotland.

Before 1297 was out the English counter-attacked. Earl Warenne contented himself with raising the sieges of Roxburgh and Berwick, but Sir Robert Clifford crossed the Solway and raided Annandale shortly before Christmas, burned a number of hamlets and defeated the Bruce tenantry in the Lochar Moss. This skirmish seems to indicate that the lord of Annandale, having lost his post in Carlisle, had gone over to the patriot side, but the facts are inconclusive. The movements of the elder Bruce after his dismissal are not known and it is not improbable that he retired quietly to his English estates leaving his headstrong son in command of his lands in Dumfriesshire. After this inconclusive manoeuvre the English withdrew from the Borders for the rest of the winter. Edward wrote from Flanders to Warenne in February 1298 stating that he intended returning to England and directing the earl not to take further action against the rebellious Scots until he, Edward, arrived to take over command.

During the ensuing months Wallace took steps to regularize his position. Towards the end of March Wallace, who had truly won his spurs at Stirling, was formerly knighted. The Rishanger chronicle does not name the earl " born of the Scottish nation " who gave him the accolade, though by a process of elimination it seems that Buchan, Carrick or Lennox were involved. About the same time Wallace was formally elected Guardian of Scotland. The situation in the spring of 1298 differed from that in which previous Guardians had governed the country. Wallace was the sole ruler and this indicated that, for a time at least, the Scots nobility, gentry and commonalty were united behind him. It has been argued, however, that such an appointment was doomed to failure; the elevation of Wallace, the younger son of a humble knight whose lord was a prominent member of the Bruce faction, was almost bound to provoke a renewal of traditional rivalries and jealousy.

At the same time Wallace incurred the implacable hatred of Edward and the English, and this may likewise have been aggravated by his relatively humble origins and meteoric rise to power. It must have been particularly galling for Edward to know that his army had been defeated in a pitched battle by the commonalty of Scotland led by a man of low rank, and on his return from Flanders the king began planning a campaign which would settle the Scottish question for once and for all. Edward transferred his government from Westminster to York, where it remained till 1304. In the early summer of 1298 he mustered a formidable army—2,000 cavalry and some 12,000 infantry (the latter mainly Irish and Welsh). The most that Wallace could pit against the English cavalry were some 200 lightly armoured horsemen, but in numbers he could match the English force near enough and be more certain of his troops' loyalty than Edward.

The English cavalry mustered at Roxburgh on 25th June. The Welsh infantry came north through Westmorland and Cumberland and joined up with the cavalry a few days later. Edward and his staff moved up from York at the end of the month, making a detour to Beverley where Edward prayed at the shrine of St. John the Evangelist and bore the saint's banner with him when he joined his army at the beginning of July. The vast army, with its attendant baggage train, moved off on 3rd July from Roxburgh in a leisurely fashion, destroying the abandoned townships on the route through Lauderdale to Edinburgh. The Scots employed a scorched earth policy, laying waste crops and driving off their cattle into the forests as they retreated before the advancing army. Edward's forces were quartered in the Edinburgh area by the middle of July. The non-arrival of the supply ships meant that the troops had to go hungry. When supplies did arrive they consisted mainly of wine, on which the Welsh bowmen got drunk and mutinous. Bishop Bek was given the task of reducing Dirleton and two other castles in the vicinity, strongly fortified by the Scots. The arrival of their rations eventually put new heart into the English who reduced Dirleton after two days fighting. The Scots made a tactical withdrawal from the other strongpoints, destroying them as they retreated to render them useless to the invaders.

Fighting actually broke out between the English knights and the Welsh infantry, and many of the latter were killed or wounded in the affray. The Welsh drew off from the main body and threatened to desert en masse to the Scots. At this point, however, Edward received intelligence reports that the Scottish army was encamped in the forest of Torwood between Falkirk and Stirling. The relative inactivity which had demoralized the English army came to an end. The cavalry saddled up and, with the reluctant infantry in tow, moved off in the direction of Linlithgow. The following morning Edward was accidentally trampled by a horse, cracking two ribs in the process, but nothing daunted he clambered painfully into the saddle and ordered his troops forward. On Slamannan Moor they paused for Bishop Bek to celebrate mass and saw, on the hillside, the Scottish army preparing for action.

Wallace's spearmen were drawn up in the formation known as the schiltrom, a hollow square of two ranks, front rank kneeling and rear rank standing, with their long spears thrust forward in formidable array. Between the schiltroms were bodies of short-bowmen, and the small cavalry force was mustered in the rear. Wallace deployed his troops to take advantage of the natural features—the marshy ground of Darnriggs in front where the Westquarter Burn and its tributary met. The deep valley of the Westquarter Burn protected his left flank to some extent, while woods and rocky escarpments protected his right.

Edward attacked in three broad formations of heavy cavalry, charging down the Ettrick bowmen in the spaces between the four great schiltroms. The bowmen were no match for the English cavalry and they broke and fled, but the spearmen stood firm and inflicted considerable damage on the English horsemen. Edward now brought up his Welsh archers, armed with their deadly weapon, the long-bow, and soon decimated the ranks of the schiltroms. The Scottish ranks wavered and then were smashed as Edward sent in the heavy cavalry again. The spearmen fought back desperately but were overwhelmed and slaughtered by the hundred. The Scottish cavalry, which included those of the nobility in support of Wallace, slipped away into the woods. The Earl of Carrick may have been present on that ill-fated day and made his escape with Wallace and the other leaders. His movements in the ensuing months are not known for certain, though he probably returned to Ayrshire soon after and organized the evacuation of Ayr and the destruction of its castle to prevent it falling into Edward's hands.

The Battle of Falkirk was in no sense decisive. The Scottish men at arms took the brunt of the English attack but the cavalry, the "officer corps", got away unscathed to fight another day, or at least organize resistance in the remoter districts, especially north of the Tay and in the hills of Galloway. It seems likely that the young Bruce took command of the guerrillas operating in Galloway in the summer of 1298. After Falkirk the English proceeded north to Stirling, sent raiding parties east to sack Perth and St. Andrews, and then retreated south to Edinburgh. The main column headed south-west across Peeblesshire and Lanarkshire to Ayr by the end of August and thence by Nithsdale to Lochmaben. On 2nd September Edward reached Treskuer (Troqueer) on the west bank of the Nith overlooking the town of Dumfries and inspected the Castledykes site south of the town itself. The following day he was at Dalgarno and Tibbers where he must have seen the stone castle built by Sir Richard Siward. On 4th September he stayed at Lochmaben where his troops occupied the Bruce mote hill by the church. The Bruce castle stood on an eminence between the Kirk and Castle Lochs dominating the main road north and south. As at Dumfries, Edward inspected the existing fortifications in some detail, his object being to establish military strongpoints for the control of Scotland against further outbreaks of rebellion. In Wales Edward had built massive fortresses in stone, designed for the permanent subjugation of that principality. In Scotland, however, he seems to have been concerned with a less permanent form of occupation, and for that reason felt that wooden peles were sufficient. Stockaded peles were subsequently erected at Selkirk and Dumfries and a similar structure at Lochmaben—but not on the site of the existing castle of Annandale.

At the southern end of the Castle Loch was a long, narrow peninsula with the remains of an Iron Age fort, the *temenos* of Maporos. Edward selected this site for a wooden pele and left Sir Robert Clifford in charge of the construction gangs. On 25th November 1298 he ordered all good men of Annandale to aid and obey Sir Robert who was appointed captain and lieutenant " to suppress the Scots enemies ". The work progressed quickly and by Christmas Day was sufficiently well advanced for Robert de Cantilope to be appointed its constable. On 28th December the work force was augmented by 48 labourers from Cumberland, " to erect a Pele at Lochmaben at a wage of twopence *per diem* ". Sawyers and carpenters were among the dozen skilled craftsmen who were subsequently drafted to finish the interior. On 2nd February 1299 Clifford wrote to the King's Treasurer at Carlisle, asking that, as he had ordered the crossbow men to remain at Lochmaben under the constable, they should receive fifteen days' pay in advance along with further crossbow men coming from Carlisle, with threepence daily each owing to " the great dearness in the country."

This pele was attacked in August 1299 by Scottish forces commanded by the Earl of Carrick, operating from the great Border castle of Caerlaverock. The attack was beaten off and Robert de Conynghame, constable of Caerlaverock, was killed in the assault. His head was subsequently displayed on a pole from the great wooden tower. Steps were taken to reinforce the original wooden structure and in November of that year Siward was instructed by Edward to strengthen " the palisade of the close of Lochmaben Castle " with stonework. In the ensuing century this was to form the nucleus of a great stone castle, strategic key to the western Borders of Scotland, and even today its ruins are an impressive reminder of its former importance. Today it is known locally as Bruce's Castle—though ironically his only connection with it was the abortive raid of 1299.

After the débâcle of Falkirk Scotland had little use for its defeated leader. Wallace resigned the guardianship; whether voluntarily or not is immaterial. His position had become increasingly untenable in face of the jealousies of his high-born colleagues and it is interesting to speculate whether he would have been removed from office ere long, even if the battle of Falkirk had been successful. For a time he fades into the background, but still a guerrilla of no mean reputation. He reemerged briefly in 1303–4 as one of the commanders in the campaign of that year, but paradoxically his immortal position in Scottish history was assured by the manner of his capture, trial and execution as a traitor in 1305.

Chapter VI

The Comyn Wars

Some time between the disaster of Falkirk and November 1298 the insurgents fell back on the old idea of a collective leadership and appointed two Guardians in the name of King John and the realm of Scotland. The choice of Guardians is an interesting one, representing the union of the two main factions. John Comyn, younger of Badenoch and nephew of King John, represented the Balliol faction. The Earl of Carrick, now twenty-four years old, represented the Bruce faction. While there was an immediate threat from England the two Guardians co-operated well enough and the day to day administration of Scotland continued reasonably smoothly. Sheriffs held their courts in many parts of the country, taxes were collected and parliament continued to meet—perhaps irregularly and in some rather unconventional locations—but acts were passed for the good governance of the country.

The dual guardianship functioned for about a year but as the threat of invasion receded the urgency which had united the factions vanished and the old rivalries came to the surface once more. In July 1299 Bishop Lamberton returned from his diplomatic missions on the Continent and was just in time to attend a meeting of the patriot leaders in the forest of Selkirk on 12th August, following a guerrilla raid on the suburbs of Edinburgh. We have a remarkable eye-witness account of that memorable meeting, a report by a spy planted by Robert Hastings, Constable of the English garrison in Roxburgh Castle. This report, now preserved in the Public Record Office in London, enumerates the leaders then present. William Wallace significantly was absent—he had gone abroad on a self-appointed diplomatic mission—but his brother Malcolm was there, and so was the Bishop of St. Andrews, a Wallace appointee. Of the earls Buchan was a Comyn and Menteith was a cousin of the Steward—a Bruce man. The Steward himself was present, and then there were two knights—David de Brechin (Buchan's nephew) and David Graham (a staunch Balliol supporter). Furthermore relations between the Earls of Buchan and Carrick had been none too cordial since the former had taken over the lands of Annandale which Carrick's father, the erstwhile Governor of Carlisle, was deemed to have forfeited. The report described the dramatic events of the meeting:

> At the council Sir David Graham demanded the land and goods of Sir William Wallace because he was leaving the kingdom without the leave or approval of the Guardians. And Sir Malcolm, Sir William's brother, answered that neither his lands nor his goods should be given away, for they were protected by the peace in which Wallace had left the kingdom, since he was leaving to work for the good of the kingdom. At this, the two knights gave the lie to each other and drew their daggers. And since Sir David Graham was of Sir John Comyn's following and Sir Malcolm Wallace of the Earl of Carrick's following, it was reported to the Earl of Buchan and John Comyn that a fight had broken out without their knowing it; and John Comyn leaped at the Earl of Carrick and seized him by the throat, and the Earl of Buchan turned on the bishop of St Andrews, declaring that treason and *lèse majesté* were being plotted. Eventually the Steward and others came between them and quietened them. At that moment a letter was brought from beyond the Firth of Forth, telling how Sir Alexander Comyn and Lachlan [MacRuari, captain of the West Highland galloglasses] were burning and devastating the district they were in, attacking the people of the Scottish nation. So it was ordained then that the Bishop of St Andrews should have all the castles in his hands as principal captain, and the Earl of Carrick and John Comyn be with him as joint-guardians of the kingdom. And that same Wednesday, after the letter had been read, they all left Peebles.

Reading between the lines, we may imagine the electrically-charged atmosphere of that meeting, the frayed tempers and the sternly moderating influence of Bishop Lamberton and the Steward. The appointment of the Bishop as a third Guardian was a wise move. Lamberton had been chancellor of Glasgow

Cathedral, a protégé of Wishart (a Bruce supporter) and Wallace (a vassel of the Steward), so his career had aligned him with the south-west of Scotland where the Bruces were strongest; but he came from a family which had roots in the north-east and his bishopric, the most important in Scotland, lay north of the Forth in country more usually associated with the Comyn family. Thus his background and position were admirably suited to make him the link-man between the two potentially warring factions, and his own strength of character would ensure that he had a restraining influence on the two young hotheads. Once more the Guardians of Scotland represented the three classes of the Establishment—the earls, the barons and the bishops.

Dissension among the leaders was probably due to military inactivity, always bad for morale in wartime. Consequently they decided on renewed action. In the ensuing period, as already noted, Bruce made his abortive attack on Lochmaben from the Maxwell stronghold of Caerlaverock. The Comyns went north while the Steward and the Earl of Menteith turned west into Lanarkshire. Lamberton remained in Selkirk Forest keeping an eye on the southern approaches. In November the three Guardians came together in Torwood during the last stages of the siege of Stirling Castle. The English garrison was being starved into submission and Edward, who had mustered a host at Berwick intent on raising the siege of Stirling, was powerless on account of the weather and the recalcitrance of his nobles, to take the field against the Scots at that time of year. On 13th November the Guardians wrote to Edward saying that Philip of France had offered to mediate on their behalf and arrange a truce. Edward, however, refused to agree to this and some sporadic fighting went on through the ensuing winter without anything decisive being achieved. The Guardians went their separate ways again, leaving Sir John de Soules to receive the submission of Stirling Castle shortly afterwards.

The events of the winter months of 1299–1300 are obscure, but some time between November and the following May the Earl of Carrick resigned as Guardian. There was a clash of personalities among the Guardians and it seems that young John Comyn was the troublemaker—at one point he declared vehemently that he would not serve with Bishop Lamberton.

The Steward and the Earl of Atholl intervened on behalf of the Bishop, but in the end it was Bruce, not Comyn, who left the board. His place was filled by Sir Ingelram de Umfraville, one of the Comyn faction and a relative of the Balliols. Robert Bruce was undoubtedly soured by this turn of events; from this period dates his disillusion with and disaffection from the patriot cause. This was compounded by military operations in the south-west, the traditional Bruce country. The Earl of Buchan (who was also sheriff of Wigtownshire) campaigned in Galloway early in the year to win over the Gallovidians, always men of an independent turn of mind, whose chief enemy was not the king of Englind but (as they saw it) the Earl of Carrick whose territories in Annandale and Ayrshire tended to encircle them. In July Edward's long-awaited invasion of Scotland got under way. Angered at the temerity of the Scots in attacking his newly founded pele of Lochmaben the previous autumn, Edward concentrated his energies first on reducing the castle of Caerlaverock at the mouth of the Nith, some ten miles south of Lochmaben. The splendid structure which dominates the Solway coast south-east of Dumfries was largely built by the Maxwells in the fifteenth century and the castle of Edward's time was a much more modest affair. According to the contemporary ballad of the siege the castle was lightly held by about sixty men. Siege engines were brought in by sea and soon made short work of the defences. According to one account the defenders were allowed to depart on terms; another states that the constable and 21 of his men were imprisoned at Newcastle and Appleby, while the Lanercost Chronicle says merely that many of the defenders were subsequently hanged. At any rate the surrender of the castle was an amusing diversion for Edward and his new bride (the sister of Philip of France, living symbol of the Treaty of Provins between English and France).

The Scots probably realized, by the scale of Edward's preparations, that he intended to subjugate the country as thoroughly as he had done four years earlier and they made overtures for peace. Bishop Dalton tried to parley with Edward but was brushed aside. At Kirkcudbright Edward met John Comyn and the Earl of Buchan and received the Scottish peace proposals—the restoration of King John and the restoration of estates in England forfeited by the Scottish magnates. Edward regarded these reasonable proposals as impertinent and brought the two-day parley to an abrupt close. The English army moved slowly forward through Galloway. While Edward tarried at Twynholm his scouts engaged a party of Scots on the Cree estuary and captured Sir Robert Keith the Marischal. The following day the main body of the English army advanced to the Cree, and paused at a point midway between the present day village of Creetown and Newton Stewart, where the river winds and loops through mud flats to the sea. On the Wigtownshire bank the Scottish army was drawn up, with a sizeable force of cavalry. At low tide the English foot soldiers forded the river and engaged the Scots at close quarter. Edward intended to hold back his cavalry but through some breakdown in communication the Earl of Hereford led his brigade forward and charged into the Scots. Edward felt obliged to follow, against his better judgment, and the entire English cavalry crossed the river. At this, however, the Scots were thrown into panic and confusion and fled in disarray. Edward did not press home his advantage, so the actual Scottish losses were light, and the English army recrossed the Cree without having achieved much.

The Scots were rather more successful on the diplomatic front. Bishop Lamberton's mission of 1298–9 at last bore fruit, in the form of a stern rebuke from Pope Boniface, delivered to Edward via the Archbishop of Canterbury no less. Desultory fighting continued in Galloway throughout the summer, but then, on 30th October, Edward granted a truce until the following Whitsun (21st May 1301) and returned to England without achieving anything beyond the seizure of Caerlaverock.

In the meantime Scotland continued to exist in its curiously semi-independent state, though there were signs that the triumvirate of Lamberton, Comyn and Umfraville was no more successful than the previous arrangements. Somewhere between December 1300 and Whitsun 1301 the guardianship of these three was dissolved and a single ruler was appointed. According to Fordoun this appointment had the personal blessing of John Balliol, still in exile in France. De Soules occupied a position midway between the Comyn-Balliol faction and the Bruces. He was related to the Comyns by marriage, but his family, with lands in Eskdale and Liddesdale, were neighbours and ancient allies of the Bruces. Though Bishop Lamberton was no longer a

Guardian he worked closely with de Soules in 1301–2 and between them they succeeded in rallying the moderates to the patriotic cause.

Shortly before Whitsun 1301 Edward's lawyers completed the task of preparing the brief in answer to the pope's strongly worded letter of the previous summer and this set out at great length, with many dubious historical references, the case for Edward's superiority over Scotland. Having delivered the brief Edward went north yet again and remained in Scotland until February 1302, but fared little better than the previous campaign. The more important towns south of the Forth were in English hands but the country districts were lightly held, if at all; north of the Forth the patriots were supreme. Edward determined to secure the valleys of the Tweed and Clyde and contain the Forest of Selkirk which had long been valuable to the resistance movement. The English army proceeded north in a two-pronged attack. The king commanded the eastern wing moving north from Berwick while his son, the Prince of Wales, commanded the right wing moving up from Carlisle into Annandale. The king's forces moved up Tweeddale, taking Selkirk and Peebles, crossed over into Clydesdale and invested Bothwell Castle in August. The great castle fell to the English a month later.

The Prince of Wales had less success, never venturing inland from the Solway coast and getting no farther than modern Stranraer. The Scots dominated the south-west and harried his army on the flanks. De Soules and Umfraville made an assault on Lochmaben pele early in September but only just failed to capture it. The Scots mustered their forces near Loudon Hill on the borders of Ayrshire and Lanarkshire and prevented Edward and the Prince of Wales from uniting their armies on the Clyde coast as planned. To be sure the Prince's troops managed to take Turnberry Castle but he was unable to quell resistance in Carrick as a whole and was forced to withdraw before the onset of winter and join his father in his headquarters at Linlithgow.

During the winter the king of France again negotiated a truce on behalf of the Scots, from 26th January till the end of November 1302, though effectively this meant that the English were unlikely to resume the offensive until the spring of 1303 at the earliest. Credit for the strength of the resistance movement in the southwest must go to the Earl of Carrick yet, when this valuable breathing space was secured for the Scots Bruce was excluded from the inner council of state, and relegated to a minor role. He had been exasperated by Comyn and then de Soules, but the last straw was probably the news from the Papal Curia of the transfer of John Balliol from the custody of the abbot of Cluny to King Philip in the summer of 1301 and the strong rumour that Philip was now sending him back to Scotland with a French army. The restoration of Balliol was the last thing Bruce wanted, fearing that his own position as Earl of Carrick and heir to Annandale would be threatened.

Shortly after the truce began in January 1302 Bruce surrendered to Sir John de St. John, the English governor of Annandale and Galloway. A document was drawn up recording his submission and giving the guarantees of Edward to safeguard Bruce's interests. After a preamble stating that the king accepts the submission of Sir Robert Bruce the younger for the sake of the good service which Robert's ancestors and family had rendered, the document goes on the promise that if Bruce were to lose his lands or suffer any disadvantage as a result of any truce or papal ordinance, the king would grant reasonable maintenance "as is proper for him". Then it continues, "And the king grants to Robert that, so far as it lies in his power, he will not be disinherited of any land which may fall to him by right from his father, in England or in Scotland." Furthermore, in the event of the throne being restored to Balliol or his son, Bruce was to be permitted to pursue any claims to his inheritance in the English courts. "If, by chance, it should happen that the right must be judged elsewhere than in the king's court, then in this case the king promises Robert assistance and counsel as before, as well as he is able to give it." It has been argued that the right referred to here was Bruce's claim to the throne, inherited from his grandfather the Competitor, but Edward would hardly concede such a right to one who had so recently been a rebel.

In May 1302 Bruce set the seal on his defection by taking up the English appointments of Sheriff of Lanark and Governor of Ayr. About the same time he remarried, taking as his second wife Elizabeth de Burgh, daughter of the Earl of Ulster (an associate of the Turnberry Band of sixteen years previously). De Burgh was one of Edward's most loyal lieutenants and this marriage may have been intended to harness Bruce more closely to the English interest. Elizabeth de Burgh, however, was the niece of Egidia, wife of the Steward, and thus the ties between the Bruce and Stewart families were strengthened. It was the marriage of Bruce's daughter Marjorie to Walter the Steward which was to found the Stewart dynasty " that cam' wi' a lass ".

In July 1302 the French army was hammered by the Flemish rebels at Courtrai and a truce was made between England and France. A powerful delegation of Scottish leaders visited the Continent later in the year to ensure that Scotland should not suffer as a result of any *rapprochement* between the two great powers. At the same time friction between Scotland's former allies, Philip and Pope Boniface, erupted into open war, resulting in the capture of the pope by the French and his subsequent death. In May 1303 the Treaty of Paris brought hostilities between France and England to an end, thereby enabling Edward to turn his attentions once more to the Scots.

In February 1303 he sent an army north, under the command of Sir John de Segrave, with Ralph Manton, cofferer of the wardrobe, as a sort of commissioner for civil affairs. The English cavalry, in three columns, penetrated the Lothians as far as Roslin, but on 24th February the Scots, led by John Comyn and Simon Fraser, ambushed the leading column, killing Manton and capturing Segrave. The second column succeeded in rescuing their commander though he was seriously wounded. The battle of Roslin was hailed by the Scots as a major victory but, on the English side, it can be seen as no more than a probe testing the strength with which rebel territory was being held.

Edward had summoned his feudal host for May and his preparations for the campaign of 1303 were astonishingly thorough and elaborate. The latest and most fiendish engines of war were transported to Scotland by sea, and the enormous prefabricated bridges towed up the east coast by ship strangely echo the Allied preparations for D-Day in 1944. Brechin Castle was taken by siege in July 1303 and Edward's army progressed as far north as Kinloss without meeting serious resistance, but the impregnable fortress of Stirling, commanded by Sir William Oliphant, was bypassed until May 1304 when Edward began its systematic bombardment. After three months Stirling Castle surrendered and its gallant garrison were lucky to escape with their lives.

The fall of Stirling Castle was the last act in the drama. In February John Comyn made his submission at Strathord near Perth and negotiated a peace settlement in his capacity as a Guardian of the Realm. In the circumstances Edward imposed quite lenient terms on the Scots. The more prominent men were sentenced to relatively short terms of exile and although their lands were forfeited they were allowed to redeem them on the payment of sums amounting to two to five years' rent. One man was excluded from these terms—William Wallace. It was six years since Wallace had wielded almost dictatorial powers, and the vindictiveness with which Edward pursued him now seems hard to understand. In 1302 Wallace is thought to have been abroad on his self-appointed diplomatic mission, while the following year he was apparently back in Scotland engaged on guerrilla raids. Early in 1304 a punitive expedition under Segrave and Clifford defeated a Scottish force under Fraser and Wallace at Happrew near Stobo in Peeblesshire and from then on Scotland's erstwhile Guardian was on the run.

Wallace had inflicted a signal defeat on the English at Stirling Bridge, and Edward never forgot or forgave him for that. In the popular mind, however, Wallace came to symbolise the brutality and savagery concommitant with guerrilla warfare. The atrocities attributed to him were exaggerated beyond belief—but Englishmen believed them unreservedly. In truth, the real crime of William Wallace was his unswerving loyalty to the spirit of Scottish independence and his dogged refusal to submit or to be a political trimmer. Edward's terms for the Scottish surrender contain a chilling reference to this symbol of the resistance: "No words of peace are to be held out to William Wallace in any circumstances whatever unless he places himself utterly and absolutely in our will . . . Sir John Comyn, Sir David Graham and Sir Simon Fraser shall exert themselves until twenty days after Christmas to capture Sir William Wallace and hand him over to the king, who will watch to see how each of them conducts himself so that he can do most favour to whoever shall capture Wallace, with regard to exile or legal claims or expiation of past misdeeds." Thus the men who had come in to the king's peace were to be his agents in tracking down and taking the one man who had defied Edward consistently.

Wallace and a small band of his followers continued to defy the English long after everyone else had submitted. He was involved in a minor engagement near Bridge of Earn in September 1304 but nothing is known of his subsequent doings until 3rd August 1305 when he was captured in the house of one Ralph Rae in Glasgow. Rae was a servant of Sir John Menteith, formerly a staunch patriot who had been won over to Edward's side and had been rewarded for his defection with the governorship of Dumbarton Castle sometime about March 1304. The English disbursed various sums of money and land in payment for the capture of Wallace; Menteith's share of the blood money is given variously as £100 or £151.

Edward's treatment of Wallace contrasts strangely from that accorded the other Scottish leaders. They had all taken an oath of fealty to Edward at some time or another; he had not. They were great noblemen; he was the younger son of an obscure knight. Wallace was taken in chains to London, a journey which took more than a fortnight to accomplish. On the evening of 22nd August he was lodged in the house of William de Leyre in the parish of Allhallows Fenchurch and the following morning he was taken in procession, with the Mayor of London, the Sheriffs and Aldermen, to Westminster Hall. Vast crowds thronged the stifling streets that summer's day to mock and jeer the man who had inspired fearful hatred in them. A crown of laurels was placed on his brow as he stood trial—an ironic allusion to Wallace's boast that one day he would be crowned at Westminster. The trial, for treason, was a farce. Wallace admitted the charges of acts of war, convening parliaments, the murder of Heselrig and other " war crimes " but denied that he had committed treason. Nevertheless treason was the most serious offence and the punishment was to be suitably severe. The judgment set forth the horrific details of the sentence, with a great deal of moralizing over them.

The sentence was executed the same day. Wallace was bound to a hurdle and dragged over the cobblestones on a circuitous route from Westminster to Smithfield—a distance of more than four miles. There he was hanged, cut down while still living, emasculated and disembowelled. His genitals and entrails were consigned to a pyre before the gallows and then, in unimaginable agony, he received the *coup de grace*—a blow from the headsman's axe. Even when life was thus extinguished the punishment continued. His heart was ripped out and consigned to the flames and his body was butchered into four pieces. A limb and portion of the trunk were sent to a prominent city for public display. One account lists Berwick, Newcastle, Perth and Stirling; another cites Aberdeen, Berwick, Newcastle and Perth. His head, mounted on a pike, was displayed on London Bridge.

In life Wallace had had a brief moment of power and glory, followed by seven years in the political wilderness, discredited but never quite defeated. Wallace in adversity became a folk hero, a cross between King Arthur and Robin Hood, and the chronicler Wyntoun could write of him " Of his gud dedis and manhad, Gret gestis, I hard say, ar made ". His death, rather than any achievement in life, assured him of immortality. The spirit of Wallace, indeed, rallied the people of Scotland. Edward committed the supreme folly of giving the Scots a martyr—and that made them a nation more surely than a decade of oppression.

CHAPTER VII

The Steps to the Throne

IN MARCH 1304 the elder Bruce, lord of Annandale died and his son, now in his thirtieth year, inherited the vast family estates in Aberdeenshire, Dumfriesshire and Essex. To this period may belong a remarkable incised stone slab, now preserved in the Town Hall of Annan, bearing the inscription "Robert de Brus Counte de Carrik et Seygnur du Val de Annand". The date 1300, incised in more shallow numerals, appears at the end of the bottom line but was obviously added at a later period. The earliest reference to this stone appears in the diary of Bishop Richard Pococke who visited Dumfriesshire in 1760 and described the ancient mote castle of Annan. Pennant, who visited Annan twelve years later, likewise described this remarkable stone and stated that it was lodged in the wall of a gentleman's garden and had been taken from the ruins of the old castle. A similar description was given by the Rev. James Monilaws in the *New Statistical Account,* published in 1837. Subsequently the stone disappeared but in July 1914 it turned up in north Devon. The stone had been removed from Annan early in the nineteenth century by the Rev. Walter Stevenson Halliday and installed in a summer house erected on his West Country property. And there it remained until the First World War when it was discovered by an antiquary and eventually repatriated to Annan. The combination of titles, Earl (Counte) of Carrick and Lord (Seygnur) of Annandale, were borne by Robert Bruce for two years, between the death of his father and his seizure of the throne.

Since 1302 Bruce had lived relatively quietly, keeping the

king's peace. He had taken part in the hunt for Wallace in 1304, though it has been argued that he did not look very hard, and in April of that year he was involved in the transportation of the siege engines in preparation for the reduction of Stirling Castle, though the correspondence relating to this operation implies a certain lack of enthusiasm on Bruce's part. It has even been stated (by Sir Herbert Maxwell in his biography of Bruce) that he took part in Edward's parliament and was present at Westminster in August 1305 when Wallace was sentenced to death. But this supposition was based on a faulty reading of Rymer's *Foedera* and the chronicle of Matthew of Westminster —the later a notoriously unreliable source.

A parliament was convened under Edward's auspices at St. Andrews in March 1304 and Robert Bruce, the new lord of Annandale was present on the occasion. With Bishop Wishart and John Moubray, Robert Bruce was selected by Edward in the spring of 1305 to advise the king on the constitutional future of " the kingdom of Scotland "—the last time Edward used this expression. These three advised the king that ten men should be elected by the Scottish community to take part in the forthcoming English parliament, to help draw up a constitution for Scotland. With Sir John de Segrave (the English commander in Lothian) and John de Sandale (Chamberlain of Scotland) the earl, the bishop and the baron convened a parliament in May at which the ten representatives were chosen. This body, representing the bishops, abbots, earls, barons and lay community, attended the Westminster parliament in September 1305. Significantly neither Bruce nor Wishart figured among these representatives and it seems probable that they preferred to stay north of the Border while the parliament met and deliberated the Ordinance for the Government of the ' Land ' of Scotland.

Edward's nephew, John of Brittany, was appointed viceroy, but on 26th October the administration was placed in the hands of a group of four—Bishop Lamberton, John de Sandale, Robert Keith and John de Kingston, pending the arrival of the viceroy. Subsequently four pairs of justices (one Scot and one Englishman) were appointed to administer the law in each of the four regions of Scotland. Englishmen were assigned to the more important sheriffdoms and offices of state. A council was established to advise the viceroy, consisting of the ten parliamentary representatives and a dozen others, including three former Guardians—Bishop Lamberton, Comyn of Badenoch and Robert Bruce. Despite this outward semblance of Scottish participation in the government the real power was concentrated in the hands of John of Brittany and his English colleagues. Scotland, to all intents and purposes, had reverted to the status of a conquered province, as it had been in 1296.

A rather ominous clause in the Ordinance of September 1305 states " Also it is agreed that the Earl of Carrick shall be commanded to put Kildrummie Castle in the keeping of such a man as he himself will be willing to answer for." This cryptic sentence appears in a section meting out terms of exile to leaders of the erstwhile resistance movement. Though the clause itself does not necessarily imply distrust on Edward's part, seen in context it immediately raises doubts. Yet Bruce was included with Lamberton in the council to advise the viceroy, so one must not read too much into this statement. In June of the previous year Bruce and Lamberton met in the abbey of Cambuskenneth, while they were actually serving with the English army besieging Stirling Castle, and formed an alliance against potential enemies, on penalty of £10,000. No mention was made of saving their faith to the king, nor was the purpose of the alliance specified. But the bond between the bishop, who had fought steadfastly for the independence of Scotland for almost a decade, and the earl who had now inherited the Bruce claim to the throne, can only be interpreted as a prelude to the next act in the drama of resistance to foreign domination. Fortunately Edward obviously never got wind of this agreement, or else he would never have appointed Lamberton as one of the four temporary guardians pending the arrival of John of Brittany in the spring of 1306.

Superficially things were quiet during the winter of 1305–6 but events were rapidly moving towards a climax which was to revolutionize Scotland for years to come. Unfortunately we know virtually nothing about those events and the part played by the principal characters in the drama. Such information as we possess comes from the chroniclers or propagandists of a later generation and the story has been embroidered with much fanciful detail which may not stand up to critical examination. The consensus of opinion is that Bruce did not enjoy the wholehearted support and trust of King Edward at this time and

Bruce, for his part, may have felt that such distrust had arisen from some document or documents seized at the time of Wallace's arrest which might have tended to incriminate him. It is true that material of this nature was in Wallace's possession at the time of his arrest, but whether it involved Bruce in any way is only a matter for conjecture.

In February 1306 the situation deteriorated. It would appear that Bruce and John Comyn had made some sort of agreement, probably that Bruce should aim for the throne with Comyn's support, and Comyn in return would get the Bruce estates. John Comyn had succeeded his father the Black Comyn of Badenoch in 1303 and it may well be that he likewise had designs on the throne rather than continue his support for his kinsman Balliol. According to tradition (and it is no more than that) the bond between Bruce and Comyn was recorded in sealed indentures. Comyn is said to have gone forthwith to Edward and revealed all. The king called Bruce into his presence, confronted him with Comyn's copy of the indenture and asked him if the seal was his. Bruce replied that he had forgotten to bring his seal with him; could he have time to go and fetch it? Edward (surprisingly!) agreed and Bruce went to his house in London to look for it. While he was there the Earl of Gloucester sent him a shilling and a pair of spurs—a colourful way of suggesting that he make a bolt. Bruce tipped the messenger with the shilling but kept the spurs—with which he goaded his horse no doubt on the long and hectic ride back to Scotland. At Dumfries he challenged Comyn for double-dealing, stabbed him before the high altar of Greyfriars Church in Dumfries—and the rest is part of folk-lore. This naive account was designed primarily to blacken the character of John Comyn in the post-Bruce era, but it attributes to Edward an innocence and trustfulness which are utterly ludicrous.

The English chroniclers give a somewhat different version. Bruce was staying at his castle in Lochmaben and sent two of his brothers across country to Dalswinton where John Comyn had his residence. Bruce asked Comyn to meet him on neutral ground, the church of the Friars Minor in Dumfries. One account states that the Bruce brothers were supposed to kill Comyn but found him so friendly that they had not the heart to strike him down, so it was left to Big Brother to deal with him. At any rate Comyn kept his ill-fated appointment with Robert Bruce in the church on 10th February. Here again the chroniclers differ radically. Walter of Guisborough says that after friendly words were exchanged Bruce suddenly turned on Comyn, accused him of betraying him to Edward, and stabbed him. Sir Thomas Grey, on the other hand, says that Bruce spoke of the unhappy plight of their country under the English yoke. "Help me to be king and you shall have my lands, or give me yours and I will help you to win the crown." Comyn refused to listen to such subversive talk, whereupon Bruce, in a fit of anger, drew his dirk and stabbed him before the high altar.

This seems to accord with the laconic report of the affray forwarded by Edward himself in a letter to the Pope written soon after the event:

> When Lamberton was made Chief Guardian, Bruce rose against King Edward as traitor, and murdered Sir John Comyn, lord of Badenoch, in the church of the Friars Minor of the town of Dumfries, by the high altar, because Sir John would not assent to the treason which Robert planned to perpetrate against the king of England, namely, to resume war against him and make himself king of Scotland.

The actual events in the church that fateful day cannot be ascertained. The Lanercost Chronicle (compiled between 1333 and 1336) states that the Red Comyn and his uncle were slain by Bruce, but mentions none of the latter's comrades. The Scalacronica written by Sir Thomas Grey about 1355 affirms that Bruce struck Comyn with his dagger and others unnamed cut him down before the altar. John Barbour's epic poem *Brus,* completed in 1375, states that Bruce met Comyn at the high altar and with laughing countenance showed him the bond; then with a knife on that very spot, reft the life out of him. "Others too were slain of much account. Nevertheless some say that the strife befell otherwise." With such vagueness relatively soon after the event it is hardly surprising at the confusion and contradiction of later accounts. John of Fordoun's *Cronica Gentis Scottorum,* compiled between 1363 and 1385, states that the wounded Comyn was laid by the friars behind the altar and when asked by them whether he could live replied that he could. "Whereupon his foes, hearing this, give him another wound and then he was taken away from this world."

The most detailed account of the killing of Comyn is given in the *Liber Pluscardensis* compiled by Maurice Buchanan in 1461—more than 150 years after the event. We are told that the friars dragged the wounded Comyn into the vestry behind the altar. " Up came James Lindesay of Kilpatrick and asked what was the matter, and, finding that he was not quite dead but only wounded, he pressed him to say if he could recover. Yes, he answered, if remedies were at once applied to him. So James Lindesay, being a cousin and very dear friend of the said Robert, as he did not want him to come to life again, wounded him more seriously than before and despatched him." Walter Bower gives the names of *two* accomplices—James Lindsay and Gilpatrik of Kirkpatrik. A manuscript dating from the mid-sixteenth century, *Extracta e variis Chronicis Scotiae,* gives the names of the murderers as James Lindsay and Roger Kirkpatrick and this information is followed in all later accounts.

Probably the incident arose spontaneously. Both Bruce and Comyn were noted for their hot temper—as witness the incident at Stobo in August 1299 when they had been at each other's throats. In an age when men of quality went about heavily armed, weapons were easily drawn and arguments settled with the point of a blade. And human life was of little account, even when the life of a nobleman was involved. Bruce no doubt regretted his impulsive act; he ran out of the church crying " I doubt I have slain the Comyn." Whereupon Roger Kirkpatrick (so the story goes) riposted, " Do you doubt? Then I shall make sure." And going back into the church he finished the job. In folklore Kirkpatrick used the Lallans expression " mak' siccar " though Sir Herbert Maxwell points out shrewdly that he would have spoken Norman French. But the pun is just as good—*pas de doubte* in answer to Bruce's *je me doubte.* Whatever the truth it is a tale edged with the black humour which adorns so many Scottish traditions.

The seriousness of this action cannot be over-emphasized. Comyn was the head of one of the most powerful families in Scotland, with connections in the highest places. John Balliol was his uncle, the Earl of Buchan his cousin and Aymer de Valence (later Earl of Pembroke) his wife's brother. Unlike the Bruces, the Comyns had adopted a consistently patriotic stance since the death of Alexander III. His father had been a

Guardian in 1286–92 and he himself had been Guardian in 1298–1300 and 1302–4. Though his role had not been conspicuously successful he had been a prominent figure in the national movement and any further uprising against the English would depend on the support of Comyn and his henchmen. By the same token, the murder of Comyn automatically alienated the Comyn faction and rendered any future rebellion by those outside that faction exceedingly difficult if not impossible.

There is one other factor which is often overlooked. The deed itself was bad enough, but the place in which it was committed could hardly have been less propitious. This was sacrilege of the very worst kind, and such an act meant that Bruce forfeited his strongest potential ally, the Church.

He had three alternatives—to submit to Edward and certain death, to flee abroad, possibly to the court of his sister in Norway, or to face up to Edward and brazen it out. On the spur of the moment, while the town of Dumfries was in confusion over the Comyn killings, Bruce and his supporters seized their opportunity. Hemingburgh states that Bruce mounted Comyn's own magnificent horse (a nice touch) and rode at the head of a column south to the castle of Dumfries. With the element of surprise on their side the Bruce party had little difficulty in taking the castle despite its strong fortifications and earthworks. The local justices were in session in the great hall and barricaded the door on Bruce's approach, but they surrendered promptly when he threatened to burn the building about their ears. Edward's constable, Sir Richard Siward, was captured and lodged in his own castle of Tibbers, then held for Bruce by Sir John de Seton. About the same time Bruce's men seized the Comyn stronghold of Dalswinton and the castles of Ayr and Rothesay. Dunaverty Castle at the southern tip of the Mull of Kintyre was occupied by the Bruce party and Robert's own castle at Loch Doon in Ayrshire was strengthened against possible counter-attack. He failed, however, to subvert Sir John Menteith, governor of Dumbarton Castle—a sad blow since this fortress controlled access to the Highlands and Ulster from the west of Scotland.

Bruce himself hurried north to Glasgow where he conferred with his old ally, Robert Wishart in whose diocese the Comyn murders had been committed. This was a tricky moment for

Bruce. He could easily have been excommunicated and handed over to the civil authorities. Instead Wishart gave Bruce his endorsement and urged his clergy to rally to the side of Bruce as if to a crusade. The alacrity with which the Church identified itself with Bruce's aims was astonishing. Wishart even produced robes suitable for a coronation and Bruce, in turn, swore a solemn oath to abide under the direction and with the assent of the clergy of Scotland to preserve and defend the liberties of the Scottish church.

Barbour in his poem states that Bruce wrote to Lamberton at Berwick informing him of Comyn's death. No doubt he also reminded him of their pact made at Cambuskenneth. Towards the end of March Lamberton, still the trusted chief executive of Edward, slipped away from Berwick in the dead of night, crossed the Forth and hastened to Scone, near Perth, for a sacred rendezvous with Bruce. At the same time Bruce grasped the nettle firmly. He actually wrote to Edward formally demanding recognition as king of Scotland. Edward wrote back demanding that Bruce surrender the castles which were now in his possession—especially those formerly held by the Comyns. Bruce retorted swiftly that he would do no such thing. He would continue to seize strong-points till Edward acceded to his demands—and if Edward refused Bruce would defend himself "with the longest stick there is".

The English chroniclers speak sourly of the ceremony which took place at Scone on Lady Day, 25th March 1306—though the enumeration of four bishops and five earls in attendance may be a slight exaggeration. The earls of Atholl, Lennox and Menteith were present, and possibly the young Earl of Mar, but the Earl of Fife, who held the hereditary right of crowning the monarch, was absent. He was still a youth and a ward of the English court. His sister Isabel, wife of the pro-English Earl of Buchan and thus related by marriage to the deceased Comyn, decided to act on behalf of her brother and hastened to Scone to take part in the ceremony. She arrived too late for the installation of King Robert on the Friday, but at a second ceremony on Palm Sunday the Countess placed a gold circlet on Bruce's head as symbol of his sovereignty. The crown was subsequently purloined by Geoffrey de Coigners, as a souvenir no doubt, but the theft was later discovered and pardoned.

Few people seem to have taken the event seriously. Even Robert's wife, when she heard the news exclaimed, "Alas, we are but King and Queen of the May." Edward's reaction, on hearing of the murder of Comyn, was one of disbelief. Later when the events of February and March were confirmed the English court seems to have treated the affair as a huge joke. Certainly the events of those two months seem wellnigh incredible. An act of unpremeditated murder, a piece of outrageous folly, had resulted in Bruce attaining his lifelong ambition and triggering off yet another phase in the struggle for independence. All the odds were stacked against him. England had six times the manpower and infinitely greater resources; all the major fortresses and strongpoints were in English hands; the country was more thoroughly under English occupation than at any time in the previous decade; and the people of Scotland were now divided as never before, with the powerful Balliol and Comyn groups ranged against Bruce and many other influential men remaining loyal to the English connection.

Having assumed the throne Robert could do little to consolidate his position. There was no time to summon a parliament or organize the administration of the country, most of which was in alien hands anyway. As early as 3rd March, in fact, the English had retaliated by recapturing Dumfries Castle, and shortly afterwards Edward appointed Aymer de Valence, the late Comyn's brother in law, as his special lieutenant in Scotland with far-reaching powers including the right to ignore the fourteenth-century equivalent of the Geneva Convention when it came to dealing with the rebels. The movement which Bruce initiated in February 1306 was probably one of the maddest ventures in the history of any country. His enemies confidently expected that he would be defeated ignominiously within eight weeks; but eight years later he was still in the fray, undaunted by many vicissitudes, and about to inflict one of the greatest defeats ever sustained by an English army. From then onwards he never looked back—but those eight years formed the man and formed the nation at whose head he had placed himself.

Chapter VIII

The King in the Heather

It is significant that the men who recaptured Dumfries Castle on the 3rd March 1306 were not Englishmen, but the men of Galloway led by Gilbert MacDouall. Bruce's actions provoked an English reaction, but also what was tantamount to a civil war, in which many of the Scots who had fought against the English in the Comyn campaigns now fought just as fiercely against Robert Bruce whom they regarded as a murderer and usurper. Considerable research has been done on those who gave their support to Bruce in the spring of 1306. Andrew Lang, the noted historian, wrote glibly that the struggle for independence was won by men of the Lowlands "in origin mainly of English descent", but this statement does not stand up to close examination. Of the 135 landed gentlemen who supported Bruce in March 1306, only 42 hailed from south of the Forth and Clyde and most of these were from the south-west, the traditional Bruce lands of Annandale and Carrick. Only fifteen were from the Border country and none at all from the Lothians. On the other hand the men of the Highlands rallied to his cause and it was in the Highlands and Islands that the resistance movement had the strongest chance of survival. The impenetrable fastnesses of the mountains and the remoteness of the Hebrides made it difficult for English flying columns to search out and destroy pockets of resistance. It is only in comparatively recent times that the contribution of "Celtic" Scotland to the struggle has been appreciated.

Meanwhile Edward took steps, both spiritual and temporal, to defeat Bruce. He wrote to Pope Clement V to complain about the conduct of the Scottish clergy. Clement was not like his predecessor Boniface. He had, prior to his elevation to the throne of St. Peter, been Archbishop of Bordeaux, a city controlled by the king of England, and he was therefore more than ready to listen to Edward, on whom he relied for support against Philip of France. Consequently Clement issued instructions to the Archbishop of Canterbury and the Bishop of Carlisle for the excommunication of Robert early in June. To their credit the Scottish clergy paid little attention to it. Admittedly, four days later Bishop Lamberton made peace proposals to Edward—but balanced this by despatching his tenantry to Bruce's army. Poor old Bishop Wishart was seized at Cupar by the English, and with Lamberton and Abbot Henry of Scone was sent in chains to prison in southern England. Only their profession saved them from a worse fate. Edward had vowed to avenge the hideous murder of the Comyns and having done so promised to give up fighting Christian men and go on a crusade. In the meantime ordinary rebels were to be hanged when they were caught, and those implicated in the Greyfriars incident were to receive the same treatment as William Wallace. One of the first to meet this end was John de Seton, indicted by Edward "as taken in Richard Siward's castle of Tibbers which he, John, was holding against the said king, for Robert Bruce a traitor, and for aiding the said Robert in killing John Comyn . . . in contempt of God and most Holy Church, and against the king's peace."

By midsummer Valence, now Earl of Pembroke, reached Perth and quartered his troops in the town. Bruce's army was at Methven a few miles distant. A showdown in the best medieval military tradition was now prepared. Bruce rode up to the walls of Perth on 18th June and challenged Valence to surrender or come out and fight. The earl declined the challenge as it was a Sunday but replied that he would be pleased to give satisfaction the following day. Bruce accepted this and led his troops off to camp for the night. While Bruce's men were relaxing, foraging for food and cooking the evening meal, Pembroke sallied out to take the Scots by surprise. Though the hand-to-hand fighting at Methven was fierce there could be no doubt as to the outcome. The Scots were put to flight. Robert Bruce was allegedly captured at one stage but managed to escape in the mêlée. Many of his staunchest comrades fared worse. Early in

August sixteen of them were hanged at Newcastle without trial, charged with killing the King's lieges at the battle and being taken in the field. Christopher de Seton, who was captured in this engagement suffered the punishment of castration and disembowelling for his part in striking down the uncle of John Comyn in Greyfriars Church.

Bruce and a handful of men fled before the English onslaught. At this point his kingship must have seemed almost laughable but anyone who thought that he was finished had not reckoned with the dour resilience of the man. Moreover, as Barrow has pointed out, the disaster of Methven was the saving of Bruce and his kingdom. Had he won according to the rules of chivalry he would have gone on to prepare a set piece with Edward himself and asuredly he would have been crushed. As it was, he had eight years in which to prepare for a set piece on ground of his own choice.

Bruce's flight took him into the wild mountainous terrain on the borders of Perthshire and Argyll, pausing only to be succoured by the abbot of Inchaffray, and then going by Lochearnside to Glendochart. At Dalry, near Tyndrum, Bruce and his followers were intercepted by John Macdougall of Argyll, cousin of John Comyn, and not surprisingly a violent opponent of Bruce. There was a sharp skirmish in which Robert and his henchmen barely escaped with their lives. The tale of the three brothers illustrates this encounter vividly. One jumped on the horse's crupper, one caught hold of the bridle and the third seized Robert's foot and tried to unhorse him. The king kept a cool head, slew his three assailants and made his escape.

The set-to at Dalry showed the dangers lurking in wait for the Bruce party. Robert decided to split his forces so that they would be more mobile, and sent the ladies in his party overland to Kildrummie Castle in Aberdeenshire where he thought they would be safe. The ladies included Christina Bruce his sister, widow of the Earl of Mar, Queen Elizabeth and his daughter the lady Marjorie. Bruce was not to see them again for eight years. The ladies were escorted by Neil Bruce, the king's brother, the Earl of Atholl, Alexander Lindsay and Robert Boyd. With some two hundred men the king made his way south towards Kintyre. They had to get across Loch Lomond, not daring to pass round it. The young James Douglas, son of Sir William le

Hardi and destined to become Bruce's great paladin, found a small, partially wrecked boat, succeeded in repairing it, and used this to ferry the men over the loch two at a time. Those who were able swam across with their gear strapped to their backs. During this long and dangerous process King Robert sat on the bank calmly reading a French romance! The rock known as Clach nam Breatann, an ancient boundary mark above the Falls of Falloch near the head of Loch Lomond, is regarded traditionally as one of Bruce's hiding places at this time.

Barbour's *Bruce* has some quaint descriptions of the flight of the king in the aftermath of Methven. His men were foraging for food in the lands of Lennox whose earl suspected them of poaching. When he accosted them he discovered their identity; they embraced and wept for joy. Lennox and his men joined their king and travelled with the band by sea to the rock fortress of Dunaverty which Robert had seized in March, no doubt against such a contingency. Here they were aided by Angus Og Macdonald, an implacable enemy of John Macdougall of Lorne. The intricacies of these clan feuds need not concern us here, but Highland vendettas help to explain why certain clans supported Bruce while others opposed him. By mid-September, however, the enemy had caught up with him, and Bruce and his supporters were forced to withdraw from Dunaverty by sea. For some time the castle held out against the English troops of Sir John de Botetourt and the galloglasses of John of Lorne. Bruce traversed the thirteen miles of sea from the Mull of Kintyre to Rathlin Island, off the Irish coast. For more than four months his movements and whereabouts were unknown. He may have wintered in Rathlin, though this island of barely six square miles within sight of Scotland seems a rather conspicuous place in which to hole up. There are tales—part of the Bruce mythology—that he spent part of the winter in Norway, or Orkney at least, and also took refuge in Eilean Donan Castle in Kintail, but none of these stories can be substantiated.

Meanwhile the royal ladies and their escort had reached Kildrummie in safety but the imminence of the Earl of Pembroke and the Prince of Wales meant that they had to flee again. The Earl of Atholl led them northwards. Perhaps they had intended a rendezvous with the king in Orkney and were then to have made the voyage across the sea to Queen Isabel's court, but they never got very far. They took refuge in the sanctuary of St. Duthac at Tain, where they were captured by William Earl of Ross, a supporter of the Balliol-Comyn faction, and sent to Edward under strong guard.

The Earl of Atholl, captured at the same time, was subsequently hanged, beheaded and burned. Neil Bruce, Robert's brother, suffered a similar fate at Berwick. Others were hanged in a more conventional manner. Perhaps that is no more than they could have expected, but Edward betrayed the vindictive side of his character in his treatment of the Bruce women. Queen Elizabeth got off surprisingly lightly, no doubt on account of her father, Richard de Burgh, who was still loyal to Edward. She was placed under house arrest at Burstwick-in-Holderness, and Christina Bruce, widow of the Earl of Mar and recently widowed a second time by the execution of Christopher de Seton, was confined in a nunnery in Lincolnshire. But for the others something special was in store. Mary Bruce, Robert's elder sister and wife of Neil Campbell, one of his closest comrades, and Isabel, the Countess of Buchan who had turned her back on her husband's family in order to crown the Scottish king, were placed in cages constructed of iron and wood and suspended from the battlements of Roxburgh and Berwick Castles. The two wretched women were kept in their cages in solitary confinement, exposed to the elements, denied all dignity or privacy (apart from a tiny " cabinet of ease ") and subjected to the mockery and abuse of idle bystanders. How long they remained there is unknown, but they survived their ordeal and finished their imprisonment in more orthodox confinement. The Countess of Buchan at any rate spent almost four years in her cage before she was transferred to the tender care of the Carmelite convent in Berwick and three years later she was put in the charge of Sir Henry Beaumont. Mary Bruce was sent to Newcastle in 1310 and liberated four years later. Edward planned the same form of captivity for the Princess Marjorie, then a lass of about twelve or thirteen, at the Tower of London but later he thought better of it and sent her to Henry Percy, who had received the earldom of Carrick from the enraged Edward, and thence she was taken to the Gilbertine nunnery at Watton in Yorkshire. She had an allowance of threepence a day for food and a clothing allowance of two thirds of a pound per annum, substantially less than the sum allowed for a knight in captivity. Marjorie, like her aunt and her step-mother, was released after the Battle of Bannockburn.

Despite the theory that Bruce spent part of the winter at his sister's court in Bergen (her husband Eirik was dead by now, and his brother Haakon on the throne) it is more probable that Bruce stayed in Rathlin or somewhere on the mainland of Ulster. When he returned to Scotland it was to the Firth of Clyde that he came, and this points to a voyage from neighbouring Ireland. As Sir Walter Scott expressed it, in his *Lord of the Isles*:

> The rebellious Scottish crew,
> Who to Rath-Erin's shelter drew
> With Carrick's outlawed chief.

Local tradition has it that Bruce took up his abode on the island in the "rycht stalwart castell", the ruins of which still bear his name. Today the ruin of Bruce's Castle is no more than a fragment of crumbling wall, six feet high at its highest point and situated on the north-eastern corner of the island. At that time the island belonged to the Bissets of the Glens, supposedly allies of Edward, though hardly the "warm adherents" claimed by Dr. Evan Barron. In January 1307 rumour had it that Bruce was lurking on an island somewhere in the western approaches to Scotland and Edward sent out a powerful English navy, based at Ayr and Skinburness in Cumberland, to scour the waters of the Firth of Clyde and the Irish coast for him. Hugh Bisset of Antrim was ordered to join in the search with as many ships as he could muster, but this does not prove that he actually did so with any enthusiasm.

The Guisborough chronicle states that Robert Bruce sent his agents from Kintyre to Carrick in November 1306 to collect his rents, and the following February he sent a squad of men to the Scottish mainland led by his brothers Thomas and Alexander. This is confirmed by the Lanercost chronicle which says that Thomas and Alexander Bruce landed at Lochryan in Galloway on 9th February with eighteen ships and a large following, including Malcolm McQuillan, Lord of Kintyre, and Reginald Crawford, an Irish kinglet. They fell into the hands of Dungal

Macdouall who executed McQuillan and Crawford and sent the Bruce brothers to Edward for his special brand of execution at Carlisle. The heads of McQuillan, Crawford and Alexander Bruce were impaled on the three gates of that town; Thomas Bruce's head was placed above the castle keep. The death of Alexander Bruce, in particular, was a sad loss. Regarded as the most brilliant graduate of Cambridge of his time, he had already risen in the ranks of the church to become Dean of Glasgow, and undoubtedly would have filled a high position in the administration of Scotland in years to come. Within a year of seizing the throne Robert had lost three of his four brothers and seen his womenfolk subjected to a barbarous imprisonment. Lesser men would have been cowed by such experiences, but not King Robert.

Synchronized with the ill-fated expedition to Lochryan was Bruce's own landing on the mainland. As a prelude to this a detachment led by James Douglas and Robert Boyd, crossed over from Rathlin to Kintyre and thence to the west coast of Arran under cover of darkness. There they intercepted a supply train en route to Brodick Castle, commanded by the John Hastings of Abergavenny who had been one of the claimants to the throne in 1290. Having seized a great amount of arms and equipment the Bruce party were joined by Robert himself. A local tradition assigns his base to the King's Caves, two miles from Blackwaterfoot. Rough hunting sketches on the walls of the caves have been ascribed to Bruce and his companions and, for good measure, the tale of Bruce and the spider has also set there—though other places claim this honour also.

A spy was sent across the Firth to the Ayrshire coast and instructed to light a fire on Turnberry Point if all seemed well. The scout discovered that Turnberry Castle was strongly held by Percy's men and therefore felt that an attempted landing would be unwise. Unfortunately someone else chanced to light a fire on the cliff-top and this misled Bruce into thinking that the coast was clear. Too late they found that the area was swarming with English troops, but nothing daunted they launched an attack on the nearby village of Turnberry and slaughtered the sleeping soldiers bivouacked there. This bloody skirmish was small consolation for the débâcle at Lochryan, but now that he was in his own land he could count on some support from his erstwhile tenantry. Christian of Carrick, a minor gentlewoman who is thought to have been Bruce's mistress, brought him forty men and others flocked to his banner in dribs and drabs. The ensuing campaign was confined to the south-west, the terrain which Bruce and his supporters knew intimately. Robert abandoned notions of set-piece battles and chivalrous confrontations and adopted a policy of guerrilla warfare: hit and run raids on isolated English outposts, harrying supply trains, the deadly blow in the dead of night, calculated to spread panic and terror among his enemies rather than secure any major tactical advantage.

At last he was facing up to the harsh realities of the situation. He had ranged against him not only a large and powerful English army holding all the strongpoints and dominating the lines of communication, but a formidable array of Scottish noblemen and their following—Ingelram de Umfraville, the erstwhile Guardian, John Menteith, betrayer of Wallace, and John Macdougall of Lorne, kinsman of the Comyns, and others. Fortunately Bruce's enemies were still conditioned to think in terms of a defensive campaign, hoping eventually to tempt Robert out into the open where their superior manpower and materiel would overwhelm him.

Bruce, however, was singularly fortunate in the men grouped around him, and none more so than James Douglas—the "Black" Douglas of Scottish and English folklore, whose activities gave him the reputation of a bogeyman supreme. Appropriately the first occasion on which Douglas demonstrated his appetite for terrorism came on Palm Sunday 1307 when he came up to his own ancestral castle at Douglas with a small band of men. Robert Clifford commanded the garrison here, but the tranquillity of Douglasdale had made him complacent and his troops slack. On that fateful morning he held a church parade, attended by the entire garrison except a sentry and the cook left behind in the castle to prepare the Sunday joint. While the Englishmen were in the parish church Douglas and his band surrounded it. Someone prematurely let out the Douglas battle cry and the English soldiers made for the door of the church. There was a desperate hand-to-hand struggle in and around the church itself, but the thirty-odd men of the garrison were slain or captured though Clifford apparently escaped. The Scots then went to the castle, rounded up the sentry and the cook, and sat down to the meal prepared for the garrison.

It would have been utterly impracticable to hold the castle, though a decade earlier that would have seemed the customary thing to do, despite the odds. The Douglas men took as much booty as they could manage to carry away, then slashed the flour sacks and smashed the casks of drink in a glorious mess in the cellar, heaping the corpses of the late garrison on top and setting fire to the mess. This frightful scene, known as the Douglas Larder, was left to strike terror into the hearts of the relieving force and demonstrate that the forces of King Robert meant business. This episode no doubt gained in the telling, and tales of the Douglas and his exploits were much needed morale boosters. Recruitment to the Bruce side was significantly stepped up.

Strong English forces were converging on the wild moors of Galloway, on the borders of Ayrshire, Wigtownshire and Kirkcudbrightshire where Bruce and his men were holed up. From the direction of Annandale came the Earl of Pembroke at the head of 4,000 men, Percy had turned inland from the Carrick coast, Sir John Botetourt and an army were moving from Lanarkshire to avenge the massacre of Clifford's garrison, in the extreme south-west the Macdoualls were bent on repeating their success at Lochryan, and John of Lorne's galloglasses were hastening south through Cunningham and Kyle to join in the manhunt.

Early in April the net closed on Bruce's band, lurking in the wilderness of Glen Trool in the shadow of the Merrick, north-east of the Cree valley. Pembroke sent 1500 men into the glen to ferret out Bruce, but all they got was a bloody nose. On the heights above wild Loch Trool Bruce spotted the English column moving along the northern shore of the loch and sent his men down in a wild charge which utterly routed the English force. Many of the troopers under Sir John de Wigtoun were chased into the loch and drowned; others were killed by the boulders which the Scots rained down on them. Only a remnant of the rearguard made good its escape. The strip of greensward on the shore of Loch Trool is known to this day as the Soldiers' Holm in memory of the English soldiers said to have been buried there. In June 1929, on the 600th anniversay of Bruce's death, a rugged boulder of grey Galloway granite was unveiled on an eminence overlooking the loch, to commemorate the first victory of Bruce over an English force. A similar monument stands in a clearing of the forest near Clatteringshaws Loch, a few miles to the east of Glen Trool. This was the scene of another bloody encounter between Bruce's men and the English the same year. Again the Scots triumphed. An incised inscription on the massive boulder implies that Bruce leant against it in repose after the battle of Raploch Moor.

The victories at Glen Trool and Raploch Moor broke the encircling net and enabled Bruce to escape Pembroke's clutches. With his troops, numbering about 300 in all, Bruce headed north by Dalmellington and Cumnock and clashed with Pembroke's main force about 10th May in the Avon valley about twenty miles inland from Ayr. Bruce's men were deployed along the ridge of the road near the curious *kopje* of Loudon Hill. On either side the ground was boggy and impassable to cavalry—like the causeway of Stirling Bridge ten years earlier. Bruce strengthened his flanks by digging a series of trenches to prevent the enemy cavalry breaking through and taking him in the rear—the first, but by no means the last occasion on which attention to ground was to be crucial to the success of the battle. Pembroke was forced to attack on a narrow front where his cavalrymen got in each other's way. The Scots, on the other hand, fought on foot with such ferocity that they beat off the English in disorder. Chaos turned to rout, as the front ranks of the English wheeled into their oncoming comrades. The English fled along the road back to Ayr with the Scots in hot pursuit. Bruce followed up his success by attacking a relieving force under Ralph de Monthermer, Earl of Gloucester, and chasing them back into Ayr.

This string of successes put new heart into the Scots and disaffection with English rule spread like wildfire. Edward, now advanced in years, lay ill in Cumberland and the Bruce propagandists capitalised on this, spreading tales of a prophecy of Merlin that when the king died the Celtic peoples (the Scots and the Welsh) would combine, attain their independence and live in peace together to the end of the world. As one king lay dying the other king waged a vigorous campaign of burning, looting and harrying English and pro-English strongholds in the south-west. At Burgh-on-Sands, on the Cumberland coast of the Solway, the 68 year-old Edward, Hammer of the Scots, passed away on 7th July, within sight of the country he had failed to tame. The old campaigner died planning a last great expedition designed to quell the Scots and his dying wish was that his remains should be borne at the head of his army in the forthcoming campaign and stay in the field until victory had been assured. His successor, now Edward II, had other ideas. The expedition got no farther than Cumnock in Ayrshire when, on 25th August, Edward II decided that he had had enough of Scotland, assigned his command to John of Brittany and returned to London with his father's corpse, duly interred in Westminster Abbey. Three years were to pass before Edward II again personally took the field against the rebellious Scots. John of Brittany lacked the spirit and decisive qualities of Pembroke; the English administration of Scotland settled down into an easy-going routine, leaving Bruce a more or less free hand to eliminate native opposition and put his house in order.

Bruce's support in the early stages of the campaign came from landless carls and broken men, fugitives from English law who had little to lose in throwing in their lot with him. Barbour is our sole authority for many tales of Bruce's exploits in this early period and while some of them are apocryphal, others have the ring of truth and serve to illustrate the hardships and dangers which were ever present. Inevitably Bruce's band would have been infiltrated by English spies. Barbour recounts how one of them, a one-eyed rascal from Carrick, managed to secure the king's confidence by professing extraordinary devotion to duty. One morning this man and his two sons waylaid the king as he passed through a wood with his page. Robert grabbed the page's bow and put an arrow through the assassin's skull, then drew his sword and cut down the two sons as they sprang at him. His presence of mind and agility with bow, dagger or sword were well-known. On another occasion his men were encircled by John of Lorne's highlanders. Robert split his troops into three bands, sending each by a different route through the forest. John of Lorne, however, had with him a bloodhound which had once belonged to Bruce and was greatly attached to him. The faithful animal picked up the scent of his former master and the enemy began to close in on the king. He ordered his men to scatter while he and one companion stood their ground. Presently five of Lorne's henchmen came upon the king and three of them set upon him. One fell under the king's deadly sword; the other two fell back and Bruce turned to the aid of his comrade sore pressed by the remaining two highlanders. Once again the skilled swordsman prevailed and both assailants fell mortally wounded.

Danger still threatened, as John of Lorne was not far behind with the bloodhound. At one point the pursuers actually caught up with him and seized him by the cloak, but he eluded their grasp by shedding his cloak. The handsome brooch with which it had been secured thus came into the hands of John of Lorne, and is preserved by his descendants to this day at Dunollie near Oban. On another occasion Bruce and his companion fell in with three armed men on the moors. They were hunting for him but apparently did not recognize him. The five men camped in a moorland bothy for the night, during which the trio realized their mistake and attacked the two fugitives. Bruce's unnamed comrade, whom Barbour inexplicably describes as his "foster-brother", was struck down, but Bruce again despatched his assailants single-handed.

One must make due allowance for the fact that Barbour was writing hagiography without subtlety and could best convey the spirit of adulation in simple tales which could be easily understood, but some of these adventures can be confirmed by family history and local place names as well as vague traditions. The tale of the widow and her three sons is a case in point. In a glen near Loch Dee lived a widow and her three sons, each by a different husband—Murdoch, McKie and MacLurg. Bruce arrived one day at the widow's house and asked her for food and shelter. She bade him enter, saying that all wayfarers were welcome for the sake of one. "And who might that be?" asked the king. "Why—none other than King Robert Bruce, the rightful King of Scots. He's hard pressed now, they tell me; but the day will come, please God, when he shall come into his own." The king identified himself and was soon set down to a hearty meal. Soon afterwards the three sons returned home and their mother commanded them to do obeisance to the king, whose staunchest adherents they were ever after. While the king was waiting for his men to muster at the appointed place, he set the brothers to test their aim with bow and arrow. Murdoch, the eldest, shot at a pair of ravens perched on a rock, transfixing them both with the same arrow. McKie shot a raven soaring overhead and brought it to earth, but MacLurg missed his mark. Some years later, when Robert's kingdom was secure, he asked the widow how he could repay her hospitality. She asked for the parcel of land between Palnure and Penkiln on the Stewartry side of the Cree estuary. The king granted this request and in time the land, some five miles long and three miles broad, was divided between the three sons—McKie of Larg, Murdoch of Cumloden and MacLurg of Kirroughtrie. Heraldry has lent its sanction to the story, the arms of Murdoch and McKie each display the ravens duly transfixed, while the scene of their marksmanship still bears the name Craigencallie—the crag of the old woman.

During the late summer of 1307 Robert Bruce began settling his score with his arch enemies, Dungal Macdouall in Galloway and John Macdougall of Lorne. The Macdoualls and their allies the MacCans were the first target for his vengeance and Bruce spent the rest of the year harrying them into submission and replenishing his victuals and supplies at their expense. Meanwhile his lieutenant James Douglas raided the English garrisons in Clydesdale and the Borders, burning castles and rendering them untenable by the enemy. John of Brittany seems to have been singularly ineffective and his troops demoralized by these attacks.

Sometime around the beginning of October Bruce switched tactics and launched a campaign in the north-east, gathering recruits as he marched across country towards his ancestral estate in the Garioch. At Inverurie, the *caput* of the Garioch, he was stricken down by illness, brought on by the stress and privations which he had endured over the past year. At the same time his position was threatened by the forces under the command of the Earl of Buchan, and Bruce's men had to evacuate their sick leader, carrying him on a litter over the hills to Drumblade. It was here, in November, with the first of winter's snow on the ground, that Buchan's troops encountered the king's men. The running fight lasted three days, but in the end the Earl of Buchan called off his forces and the Bruce party withdrew in good order. Bruce began to get over his illness and his men brought him back to Inverurie in search of food. Buchan's army camped at Old Meldrum on 23rd December, intent on taking the king; but Sir David de Brechin and a troop of cavalry prematurely attacked the Bruce camp and goaded the sick king into a counter-attack. The appearance of the king on a horse at the head of his troops was so unexpected that Buchan's men panicked and fled. The Earl himself got away to the dubious safety of England where he died within the year; but his territory suffered grievously at the hands of Bruce's men. The Herschip (or harrying) of Buchan passed into history as an act of systematic terrorism on a level with the sack of Berwick eleven years earlier. This one-time Comyn stronghold was deliberately ravaged and devastated. It took two generations to recover and then only after it had been colonized by lowlanders loyal to the Bruce connection.

Early in the New Year Bruce turned westward, campaigning in Moray, Inverness-shire and Ross. In vain did the Earl of Ross write to his master in London seeking aid against Bruce, who had generously given him a truce till 2nd June 1308 in the hope that he would submit peacefully. In fact he held out until the end of October but nevertheless Robert dealt with him generously, granting him his lands and some other estates besides, in exchange for his promise to serve the king well and faithfully. Bruce's confidence in Earl William turned out to be fully justified. In the latter part of the northern campaign, Bruce delegated the fighting to his lieutenants and turned his attention once more to the troublesome west.

During the early part of 1308 his forces had been probing the defences of the western highlands, the stronghold of John of Lorne. Some time in April or May of that year John wrote to Edward II, in much the same vein as William of Ross, and with the same negative result. John was further hampered in that he, like Bruce, had suffered illness from which he was only just recovering at his castle of Dunstaffnage. King Robert came down the Great Glen from Inverness and confronted the men of Lorne with a force which grew daily in strength as the gentry of Argyll went over to his side. The truce came to an end in August and some time between the 15th and 23rd Robert launched an attack on the lands of Lorne.

Bruce's army came down the narrow Pass of Brander between

the precipitous flank of Ben Cruachan and the long arm of Loch Awe. John of Lorne had placed men among the crags of Cruachan to ambush the king's column and is said to have watched the progress of events from a galley moored in the loch. Bruce, however, was too wily to be caught in a situation suspiciously like the fracas at Glen Trool and sent Douglas with a party of nimble highlanders higher up the mountainside to forestall any such ambush. When the men of Lorne began to roll boulders down on the main column they, in turn, were surprised to find a party of archers on the heights above them and, being taken in the rear, they panicked and fled, making for the only bridge across the river Awe. The main column, however, forestalled them and prevented the men of Lorne from destroying the bridge. The royal army crossed in safety and promptly invested Dunstaffnage Castle, which John's aged father Alexander Macdougall was unable to defend for long. Alexander subsequently attended Bruce's parliament in March 1309 but later fled to England and died there in 1310. John of Lorne continued to hold out against the king, defending the castle of Loch Awe (identified as Inchconnell) for some months before fleeing to England like his father. For the remaining seven years of his life John of Lorne served in the councils of Edward II, holding the high-sounding title of Admiral of the Western Isles.

During the summer of 1308 Robert's sole surviving brother, Edward Bruce, carried on the campaign against the men of Galloway. In this he had a fair measure of success, completing the subjugation of the Macdoualls and the MacCans and wreaking a terrible vengeance for the deaths of his brothers. But though the Bruce armies were by now much stronger they yet lacked the equipment necessary to reduce the great English castles by siege, and the fortresses which stretched across the south-west from Caerlaverock to Ayr continued to hold fast for Edward II until 1309–10. The main achievement of 1308 was the elimination of the Balliol-Comyn faction and its adherents. The civil war of that year was an ugly episode in the Bruce war of independence, when Scot fought Scot and no quarter was given. It was, unfortunately, a necessary means to an end.

CHAPTER IX

The End of the Beginning

BY THE END of 1308 Robert had two thirds of Scotland under his control. Although Banff Castle continued to resist all the other Scottish-held castles north of the Tay had surrendered to him, and the first major English strongpoint, at Forfar, was taken by surprise on Christmas Day. Bruce's domains stretched from the Tay to the Pentland Firth and westwards to include Kintyre, Morvern and the Western Isles. Although Douglas and Edward Bruce had had some spectacular successes in the south and south-west the English continued to hold all the strongpoints. The next phase in the struggle for independence would therefore be conducted south of the Tay.

From the latter part of 1308 we have the first documentary evidence of settled government under Bruce, ordinances dated at Inchmahome, Dunkeld and Perth between September and mid-October. On 16th March 1309 a parliament—the first of his reign—was convened at St. Andrews and was attended by an impressive gathering of Scottish noblemen and clergy. Eighteen years had elapsed since a free Scottish assembly of this sort had taken place. Apart from the king himself, who still held the earldom of Carrick, three earls were present—Lennox, Ross and Sutherland. The earls of Caithness and Menteith were minors, Buchan was dead and the earls of Angus, Strathearn Atholl and Dunbar were pro-English at that time. Among the close aherents of King Robert were his brother Edward, now Lord of Galloway, Thomas Randolph, son of his half-sister and now Lord of Nithsdale, James the Steward, James Douglas, Neil Campbell and Alexander Fraser, brother of the late Simon

Fraser and the future second husband of Mary Bruce. Gilbert Hay the Constable and Robert Keith the Marischal had recently returned to the patriot side. The chief business of this parliament was discussion of a letter received from Philip of France and the resumption of Franco-Scottish relations.

The opportunity was also taken, however, to regularize Robert's position. Three years had elapsed since his double coronation at Scone—three years in which he had proved his generalship and the ability to bring the country together as none of the Guardians, not even Wallace himself, had done. On 16th March the bishops, abbots, priors and other clergy of Scotland met to give their endorsement to a declaration of right on behalf of Scottish independence and of Robert's claim to be King of Scots. The declaration stated unequivocally that Edward I of England had put John Balliol on the throne despite the fact that Robert the Competitor had the stronger claim. The document cited the trials and tribulations of Scotland under the regime of Toom Tabard, the subsequent defiance of Edward, the English invasion and the imprisonment of the erstwhile king. The events of the years between 1296 and 1306 were telescoped and glossed over. "The people, not wishing any longer to bear the calamities which had been brought upon them through want of a captain and faithful leader, had taken for their king Robert Bruce, grandson of the Competitor, and had raised him to the throne." Significantly the document ends on a wary note, as if anticipating trouble: "If anyone, in opposition, should claim right to the Scottish kingdom by means of documents sealed in the past and containing the consent of the people, be it known that all this was effected by irresistible force and violence, by manifold fears, bodily torture and other terrors, which could well pervert the opinions and minds of righteous men and strike fear into the stoutest hearts." In this remarkable document we see the earliest fruits of the Bruce propaganda that Balliol was a puppet king who had no right to be on the throne and was kept there solely by English force of arms.

The assent of the nobility carried scarcely less weight than that of the clergy, and for that reason a similar manifesto, a vote of confidence as it were, was drawn up on behalf of the earls, barons and other secular leaders. The simpler phrase "the community of the realm" gave way in these documents to the more verbose form "the inhabitants of the whole realm of Scotland acknowledging allegiance to King Robert"—an admission that there were large sections of the community which did not, as yet, owe allegiance to Bruce.

The year 1309 marks a step forward in the administrative, judicial, economic and diplomatic activity of the Bruce regime, but on the military front there was little of importance. Desultory negotiations with the English for a truce dragged on into the summer and this caused a lull in hostilities. This does not mean, however, that Robert was content to leave the English garrisons alone. His policy during the ensuing four years was one of continual harassment, guerrilla raids on outposts and ambushes of small troop formations moving through wild countryside. Whenever his forces succeeded in taking an English castle, as at Forfar, they systematically destroyed its equipment, filled in its wells and dismantled the fortifications as best they could. Whenever the English attempted retaliation and sent a punitive expedition against the Scots Bruce relied on the drastic but effective method of scorched earth—denying the enemy shelter or food by burning all houses and huts and driving off the cattle at the approach of the English. The Scottish strategy in the years from 1309 to 1314 was based on the concept of a war of attrition—to make the English realize that no matter how much manpower and materiel they poured into Scotland they could never hope to hold the country down; to make them realize sooner or later that no amount of effort would win them the war and they might as well extricate themselves and leave Scotland to the Scots. It was, after all, a poor country with a peasant economy and no great natural resources, market for English goods or even strategic importance. Given a resolute leader, time was on the side of the Scots. Like the Americans in Vietnam the English in Scotland would eventually have come to the conclusion that the country was not worth the bother. It is interesting to conjecture whether this would have been the result, whether Bannockburn was fought or not. Certainly, after the débacle at Methven in 1306, King Robert avoided set-piece battles and was confident of ultimate victory without a major showdown in the field.

For the moment Robert confined his military action to mopping up the pockets of anti-Bruce resistance which still remained in Galloway and the south-west. Wisely he left Lothian alone, for this was where the bulk of English forces were concentrated. Robert campaigned in the north and west, seeking out the supporters of the hapless John of Lorne, while his brother Edward completed the subjugation of Galloway and inflicted a sharp defeat on Aymer de St. John, routing a column of 1500 English troops with a squadron of 50 cavalry.

The protracted truce collapsed at midsummer and by the end of July Edward was at last thinking of another campaign against the Scots. His two years on the English throne had been none too happy. He had had trouble with his barons, had been forced to send his favourite, the petulant Piers Gaveston, to Ireland, had bickered with his father-in-law, Philip of France, and made himself thoroughly unpopular with his subjects. By July 1309, however, he had patched up his quarrel with his barons and appeased his parliament. Even Gaveston had been allowed to return from exile. As a prelude to active military operations Edward even got around to reinforcing the garrisons in the main castles—Berwick, Roxburgh, Dumfries, Edinburgh, Linlithgow, Stirling, Dundee and Perth. Despite these preparations Edward was still inclined to parley. He sent Richard de Burgh, Bruce's father-in-law, to negotiate with the Scots and they, in turn, sent Neil Campbell and John de Menteith to discuss peace terms with the English. The talks broke down over the question of the recognition of Robert as King of Scots, and the mobilization of the English forces continued in its leisurely fashion. It was late autumn before the English army moved north, in two great columns heading for Carlisle and Berwick respectively. Having reached these headquarters, however, the English commanders, Segrave, Hereford, Clifford and Cromwell, decided that a winter campaign in the bogs of Scotland was not a pleasant prospect and promptly made a truce with the Scots until 14th January 1310—knowing full well that no army in its right mind would commence operations at that unseasonable time of year.

By the beginning of 1310, moreover, Edward's troubles with his barons had broken out again, so the truce was extended till March, but by then he had been humiliated by the famous Armed Parliament into allowing a form of regency, the Lords Ordainers, and the truce had to be extended again until June.

A few weeks later, to be sure, writs were sent to 42 English seaports, ordering them to prepare an armada for the invasion of Scotland. Edward went north, reached Berwick in late August, quarrelled with his generals and did not commence operations till mid-September. By 20th September Edward was at Roxburgh; from there he edged cautiously westward towards upper Clydesdale and reached Biggar on 1st October where he remained for a fortnight. Famine in southern Scotland that summer had been a source of great anxiety to the Bruce government, but now it seemed a blessing in disguise for the English could find no food as they foraged in the bleak countryside. The Scottish army was content for the moment to remain north of the Forth and Clyde and leave the south to the English. Edward's troops progressed down the Clyde valley as far as Renfrew, crossed the estuary near Dumbarton and marched along the line of the Campsies eastward to Linlithgow without engaging the enemy, though stragglers on the English side were harried ceaselessly by the guerrillas led by Douglas and Edward Bruce.

Frustrated by this lack of positive action, the English army lost its impetus and Edward decided to return to Berwick till the following spring. At the end of October the English army wheeled south. The Scottish army then struck at the English rearguard, inflicting considerable damage. Edward turned to deal with this menace but the Scots vanished whence they came. Baffled and enraged by this inconclusive campaign Edward took up his winter quarters at Berwick. His battle fleet fared little better, having suffered several encounters with Scottish privateers. As a diversion Robert now planned a feint at the Isle of Man and contrived to let his plans fall into Edward's hands. Edward rose to the bait, transferred his shipping from the North Sea to the Irish Sea to deal with this threat and thereby further weakened his lines of communications.

At the season of goodwill to all men Edward despatched two envoys to Robert at Selkirk, arranging for further talks at Melrose. Robert, however, got wind of some treachery and failed to keep the rendezvous. Instead he launched a counter-attack at the beginning of February 1311, striking through Galloway and Annandale and raiding Northumberland. The campaign of 1310–11 must be judged as a victory for the Scots.

(*above*) Bothwell Castle, Lanarkshire; (*below*) Dunfermline Abbey: the tower bears the inscription "KING ROBERT THE BRUCE"

(*right*) Statue of Bruce at Edinburgh Castle, erected in 1929 on the 600th anniversary of his death. (*below*) Tomb of King Robert Bruce in Dunfermline Abbey

The English army had traversed much of southern Scotland and achieved nothing: no battles had been fought, no Scottish strongholds captured. On the other hand the English army had suffered demoralization at the hands of the Scots. Edward's troops were cold, hungry and exceedingly war-weary by the time they got back to Berwick. Naval operations on the English side had been a fiasco. On the other hand, the Scots had been dreading an English invasion on the lines of those for which Edward I had won his nickname of Hammer of the Scots. The Scots had braced themselves for an onslaught, but none had materialized, and there was something particularly exhilarating in harrying a dejected English army retreating back to Berwick. The victory was therefore moral, rather than material.

A similar pattern was repeated in 1311. The bulk of the English army remained at Berwick, a constant threat to the Scots, but Edward and Gaveston were forced by the intransigent attitude of parliament to return to London, whereupon Gaveston was sent into exile a second time. As soon as Edward departed for the south Robert's army in Annandale struck. Crossing the Solway and the Sark the Scots raided deep into Northumberland, sacking the town of Haltwhistle in Tynedale before retiring in good order. This lightning strike was no more than a probe of the English defences. Its success limited though it was, encouraged the Scots to raid the north of England later in the year. In September they swept down from the hills along the Border and ravaged Redesdale. This raid lasted fourteen days and inflicted heavy damage, looting and burning crops at harvest time. The Northumbrians decided to buy off their attackers and offered £2,000 sterling—an enormous sum for those times—in exchange for a truce lasting till Christmas.

Edward resolved to take action against the Scots in January 1312, but only got as far as York this time before his chronic constitutional troubles erupted anew. This time it was his cousin, the Earl of Lancaster, who headed the nobles opposed to him. Edward remained at York until April, using Lamberton (recently released from prison) and the Earl of Atholl to negotiate a prolongation of the truce with the Scots. As before, however, Robert would not consider a lasting peace until the English agreed to recognize him as the rightful king of Scots.

Although there was no large scale fighting in 1312 the Scots gave serious attention to reducing the English strongholds in their midst. At the end of 1311 the English garrison holding Bruce's own castle in Loch Doon was forced to surrender. Edward Bruce laid siege to Dundee, cutting off the supply lines by sea and reducing the English garrison to the point of starvation. Eventually the commander, Montfitchet, agreed to surrender if he was not relieved by a certain time and sent word to Edward appealing for reinforcements and supplies. Edward ordered Montfitchet to hang on, threatening him with death and forfeiture if he failed, but without sending him the provisions he so desperately needed. Not surprisingly Dundee fell to the Scots some time in the spring of 1312.

Perhaps goaded into action at last by the fall of Dundee, Edward moved up from York to Newcastle in April but realizing the futility of operations at that time he soon returned to York, where domestic problems again preoccupied him. In June the Earl of Lancaster seized Gaveston and had him beheaded. Stung by this act of defiance, Edward took his army south to deal with his rebellious nobles and Scotland was again relieved of the threat of invasion.

That the south-west was now secure is demonstrated by the fact that Robert was able to hold his parliament at Ayr in July. Ayr, formerly one of the strongest English centres in Scotland, was now to become the advance headquarters for the Scottish campaign against the English-held Borders. Originally Robert intended to tackle the English castles at Buittle, Dumfries and Caerlaverock, leaving his brother to lead the main force into Northumberland; but in August he decided to bypass the castles for the time being and harry the north of England in full strength. This time the English tasted the ferocity of a full-scale Scottish invasion. The Scots ravaged Lanercost, burned Hexham and Corbridge, took Chester-le-Street and sacked Durham itself. The leading gentry of the county met Robert Bruce himself at Hexham on 16th August and bought a truce till midsummer 1313 for the sum of 2,000 marks, payable in instalments. Similar examples of blackmail (here used in its strict sense) were arranged by the citizens of the other northern counties—and also by the Scots of Lothian supposedly living under English protection. When midsummer 1313 approached Robert let the northern English counties know that the deadline was near and offered them a continuance of the truce under the same monetary terms. In most cases this threat was sufficient, but when Cumberland had failed to pay up by April 1314 the Scots led by Edward Bruce ravaged the countryside for several days to teach the Cumbrians a lesson. This situation continued for several years as the Scots gradually liberated their own country. The money, cattle and foodstuffs taken by the Scots from the four northern counties of England amounted to many thousands of pounds and provided a steady source of revenue to the Scottish exchequer. Scotland's gain was England's loss; during the same period the northern counties were virtually exempt from taxes and the English revenue suffered accordingly. It has been estimated that the money paid to Robert was twice, or even thrice the amount which would have gone to the English treasury. At one stage the palatinate of Durham was forced not only to pay heavily for immunity from Scottish attack, but also had to permit the free passage of Scottish troops across its territory—so that they could launch an attack on Yorkshire, hitherto free from Scottish raids!

Meanwhile Robert improved his position on the diplomatic front. In October 1312 he went north to Inverness, leaving Edward Bruce and James Douglas to conduct the campaign in the south. At Inverness he convened a parliament whose main business seems to have been the negotiation of a treaty with Norway, tantamount to the recognition by a European power of the sovereignty of Scotland and the kingship of Robert. Although full diplomatic relations with the German cities and the Low Countries were not resumed for some years a practical working relationship already existed. Scottish wool was much in demand on the Continent and the merchants of the Hanseatic towns continued to trade with the Scots throughout this period, using Inverness and Aberdeen as the main ports. As the war with England progressed the German and Flemish merchants came out more openly in support of the Scots, giving a haven to Scottish ships when they were hard pressed, and even impounding English ships and cargoes on occasion.

Towards the end of 1312 Robert turned his attention to the English castles which yet remained in Scotland. On 6th December the Scots made an assault on Berwick but failed to dislodge the garrison. Nevertheless this attack demonstrates

Bruce's confidence and the aggressive spirit of his lieutenants. It also indicates a change in tactics, from the essentially guerrilla warfare of the earlier period to a willingness to take on the English, even when the latter were in strong defensive positions. The attack on Berwick was skilfully prepared and began with the element of surprise which was the hallmark of Douglas's operations. Special scaling-ladders with hooks to grip the stonework and sockets in the hooks to permit their lifting on spear-point, were placed against the wall. The assault party actually got to the top of the ramparts when a dog barked and gave the alarm and the marauders were forced to withdraw.

On 8th January 1313, however, Perth, the most important English stronghold north of the Forth, fell to the Scots after a seven weeks' siege. Ironically the commander of the Perth garrison was none other than Sir William Oliphant, whose gallant defence of Stirling Castle on behalf of John Balliol has already been mentioned. Oliphant had spent four years (1304–8) in English prisons before being released on condition that he would serve against Bruce. Since the late summer of 1311 he had been in command of Perth, having taken over from the luckless Gaveston, and from then onward the town had been more or less under constant Scottish attack. The town was wellnigh impregnable, being ringed about by massive walls and a system of canals linked to the River Tay. Although the Scots had effectively cut off the town from outside help it was cunning rather than force of arms which led to its capture. On the murky night of 7th–8th January the Scots managed to give the impression that they were moving off when, in fact, they were swimming across the icy waters of the moat with their special scaling-ladders—led by none other than King Robert himself. Robert is said to have been the second man over the top of the ramparts—to the utter astonishment of the defenders who surrendered with scarcely any resistance. It was individual acts of bravery (almost braggadocio) which endeared King Robert to his people. Undoubtedly Robert combined the qualities of good generalship with a certain flair for showmanship. The English troops were permitted to leave under terms; a few of the leading citizens were summarily executed *pour encourager les autres* but generally speaking the capture of Perth was a bloodless affair. A month later Robert was back in the south-west, conducting the siege of Dumfries Castle which was held for the English by his old enemy, Dungal Macdouall of Galloway. The castle was starved into submission on 7th February but curiously enough Robert left Macdouall go free—to fight for Edward another day. Caerlaverock and Dalswinton fell to the Bruces about the same time, and the old Balliol stronghold of Buittle capitulated by the end of March.

Outside Lothian there remained but two strongholds in English hands—Bothwell on the Clyde, which managed to hold out for a further year, and Stirling which had been strongly garrisoned by the English since 1304. Edward Bruce was given the task of reducing Stirling. Sieges of this sort were none too congenial to him. His conduct of the sieges of the Galloway and Dumfriesshire castles the previous summer had not gone according to Robert's liking and he had personally relieved his brother of the command. Now Edward Bruce had the chance to redeem himself by capturing the greatest prize of them all. Edward laid siege to Stirling Castle from Lent to Midsummer 1313 without success and then did a deal with its commander, the Scottish knight Philip Moubray. If no help appeared within three miles of Stirling by Midsummer 1314 Moubray promised to surrender the castle without any further fight. Impetuously Edward Bruce agreed to this astonishing proposal. Perhaps he felt that the likelihood of Edward sending help was remote, judging by his past performance. Unfortunately the agreement was too well-publicized and the goal too precious for Edward II to ignore the challenge and he began making elaborate preparations for a campaign designed to raise the siege of Stirling within the stated period. He patched up his quarrel with his nobles and convinced them that England could not stand by, with the whole world looking on, and let Stirling go without a fight.

Robert Bruce immediately recognized the danger inherent in this situation and reprimanded his brother for his reckless display of chivalry. There was no time to be lost, however; the showdown which had been avoided for so long could not be put off much longer. While Edward II began raising the most impressive army seen in England for almost twenty years Robert made a desperate effort to reduce the other English garrisons while there was still time.

Linlithgow Castle, long a favourite English base, fell to the

Scots in September 1313. A local farmer named William Binnock held the contract to supply the garrison with hay and one day he promised them a load of exceptional quality. He was as good as his word. On the appointed day he drove his cart up to the castle gate and the portcullis was raised to let him through. The cart was parked in the gateway while William and his driver dealt with the porter. The portcullis was lowered hastily by the guard and jammed on the hay-cart, whereupon Binnock's accomplices, lurking outside, rushed in and grappled with the garrison which was swiftly overpowered. The interesting point about this anecdote is that the castle seems to have been seized on the initiative of local resistance fighters, of humble birth at that, and illustrates the fact that the people of Lothian were not content to sit back any longer under foreign domination, but were prepared to join in the national struggle.

On Shrove Tuesday 1314, while the garrison was feasting, Roxburgh Castle was attacked by Douglas using the now familiar method of grappling hooks and rope ladders. The English were taken by surprise and surrendered with little resistance. On 14th March Thomas Randolph led the assault on Edinburgh Castle, a formidable obstacle atop its towering rock. A diversionary assault took place at the East Port—the only obvious place for an attack—and this held the attention of the defenders while Randolph's cragsmen, led by William Francis who knew of secret paths up the cliff face, scaled the heights and took the garrison in the rear. Having overpowered the guard the climbers opened the gates and Randolph's main force swarmed into the castle. Most of the garrison were slaughtered, but their commander, a Gascon knight named Pierre Liboud, defected to the Scots. Bruce had little use for him and subsequently he was executed for treachery.

There remains one other sideshow to be mentioned before we come to the main act in the drama. Ever since Bruce had taken refuge at the beginning of his reign on the island of Rathlin, Ireland had been involved to some extent in the Anglo-Scottish struggle. Richard de Burgh, Earl of Ulster was in an invidious position, as trusted lieutenant of the English king, but also as Robert's father-in-law. At various times he seems to have been employed cynically by both Edward and Robert as a sort of go-between. As the Scottish position became stronger and

Edward's situation fluctuated (depending on the state of his relations with his baronage and parliament) Ulster's attitude towards the Scots varied from armed neutrality to active friendship. By the middle of 1310 at least, Scottish trade with Ireland had been re-established and undoubtedly much of the sinews of war, both foodstuffs and military equipment, were finding their way from Ireland to the Scots. We have already seen how John of Lorne was appointed by Edward as Admiral of the Western Isles. This may have been no sinecure. There is some evidence to suggest that he operated a fleet of galleys from a base on the Irish coast (probably Dublin or Drogheda) with the purpose of harrying the Scottish islands and disrupting merchant shipping between Ulster and the west of Scotland.

One place which seems to have obvious strategic significance is the Isle of Man, more or less equidistant from Scotland, England and Ireland. The island had been part of the Scottish realm from 1266 till 1290 when Edward I had quietly purloined it. Robert threatened to invade it in 1310 but some years passed before this was accomplished. The exact date of the Scottish invasion of Man is not known; various dates between May 1313 and July 1314 have been given, and the latter seems more likely. The Scots, commanded by the king, landed on the east coast and seized Castle Rushen, the island's main fortress, but it was captured by John of Lorne in 1315, acting in the English interest. It was in Scottish hands again from 1317 till 1333 but then, like Berwick, passed from Scottish control for good.

Chapter X

Bannockburn

At the beginning of 1314 Robert Bruce's star was in the ascendant. At his back he had a united people and a country which was all but freed of foreign domination. Only five castles remained in English hands and all but two had capitulated by Midsummer's Day. On the other hand Scotland had been impoverished by eighteen years of warfare and nine major English invasions. Abroad she had the friendship of Norway and the commercial interests of Germany and the Low Countries, but Clement V was not the friend that Boniface VIII had been, while Philip of France could no longer afford to quarrel with his son-in-law and was therefore unlikely to help the Scots against Edward II. To be sure, Edward had had his internal disputes to contend with, but Bruce had fought a bitter civil war to secure *his* position, and there were still many Scots, like the Earl of Dunbar and Ingelram de Umfraville, who preferred service to England rather than submitting to a Bruce usurper. In manpower alone England probably outnumbered Scotland five to one; but, with the exception of the four northern counties, England had not felt the hardships of war and was one of the most prosperous countries in fourteenth-century Europe. Diplomatically England was in a strong position. Ireland and Wales were at peace, there was a lull in the struggle with France, relations with the Empire and the Papacy were cordial, and Edward maintained close links with many European courts. Internally England was more peaceful than at any time since the accession of Edward II seven years earlier. The murder of Piers Gaveston had shamed many of Edward's opponents into patching up their quarrel with him. In the spring of 1314 the earls and barons of England were—nominally at least—united behind their king.

At the end of November 1313 Edward wrote to the Earl of Dunbar promising that he would come north the following summer with an army for the pacification of Scotland. Shortly before Christmas Edward sent writs to eight earls and 87 barons summoning them and their men to Berwick on 10th June 1314. In February Edward reiterated his plans and gave some detail of his strategy, which was to be based mainly on infantry. In March these plans were implemented by the executive orders for the mobilization of men and equipment. Virtually every English seaport was ordered to provide ships to transport the supplies and equipment needed by the land forces, and also to bring troops over from Ireland. The Earl of Ulster took charge of the Irish operations, but it is not known to what extent either the Anglo-Irish nobility or the native Irish chiefs actually obeyed the summons. About 16,000 infantry were conscripted from the thirteen counties in the north and midlands, and a further 5,000 from Wales—long-bowmen, crossbowmen and spearmen which Edward intended as his main fighting force. Various estimates of the cavalry have been made, but the consensus of opinion is that about 2,500 knights, esquires and mounted men-at-arms eventually took the field. Edward's preparations in the spring of 1314 were well-publicized and individual knights and soldiers of fortune flocked to his banner from all over Europe. In manpower, arms and equipment the English army of 1314 was a formidable force, but doubts have been cast on its training and leadership to explain the subsequent débacle. Although Edward lacked the generalship of his father he possessed great personal courage. In his chief lieutenant, Aymer de Valence, Earl of Pembroke, he had one of the ablest soldiers of his time, with an unrivalled knowledge of campaigning in Scotland over the previous decade. Pembroke had clashed with Bruce twice before, winning once (Methven) and losing once (Loudon Hill) and he no doubt felt confident that this would be a case of third time lucky. The subordinate commanders included Humphrey de Bohun, Earl of Hereford, Sir Marmaduke Tweng and Sir Robert de Clifford—all seasoned veterans of the Scottish wars—and also Sir Ingelram de Umfraville, who had fought bravely on the patriot side against the English in the Comyn campaigns.

Barbour says that King Robert's army was about a third the size of the English force and this seems to agree with the estimates of 6,000 to 7,000 foot soldiers calculated from other sources. In equipment the Scottish infantry was lighter clad and less well armed than their opponents, relying on spears and axes and a sprinkling of short bows. Robert's cavalry, commanded by Sir Robert Keith, could not have amounted to more than 500 men lightly mounted and no match for the formidable destriers used by the English.

As the English preparations drew to their climax the Scots mustered their army at Torwood south of Stirling. In the vicinity were the locations of two previous battles on a grand scale—Stirling Bridge to the north and Falkirk to the south. Twice before the fortunes of Scotland had waxed and waned as a result of a battle in this area. Now, both Robert and Edward must have realized that their personal careers were at stake, as well as the future of their respective countries—with the Scots inevitably losing more by defeat than the English. This thought alone, however, would have stiffened the Scottish will to succeed; and, in addition, the morale of the Scots was aggressively high, thanks to the exploits of Edward Bruce, Douglas, Randolph and the king himself. Robert Bruce was approaching his fortieth birthday: Edward II had just passed his thirtieth. The ten year gap in the ages of the respective leaders should not be discounted. Robert was in his prime, a man of maturity hardened by adversity. Edward, however, was immature in many respects, displaying a petulance and waywardness surprising in the son of such a father. At times highly irresponsible in his actions, at best he approached the job in hand with a perfunctory, almost absent-minded, manner. Robert, on the other hand, had a keen eye for detail and a meticulous sense of preparation. If he was forced to face the English in the field, it would be a field of his own choosing and one which was well prepared for the event.

The venue of the Scottish assembly was well chosen. In May Edward relayed intelligence reports of the Scottish muster at Torwood to his sheriffs: "The Scots are striving to assemble great numbers of foot in strong and marshy places, extremely hard for cavalry to penetrate, between us and our castle of

Stirling." The Torwood straddled the highway from Falkirk to Stirling. As its name suggests, it was an area of tors, or rocky outcrops, heavily wooded. To the west lay rocky hills, to the east the marshlands near the Forth estuary. To the north lay further marshland, partially drained by an insignificant stream named the Bannock Burn.

On 17th June, exactly a week before Midsummer's Day and the deadline for the surrender of Stirling Castle, Edward's army left Berwick and headed north, through Lauderdale towards Edinburgh. It must have been an impressive sight—the squadrons of gaily-caparisoned destriers, the serried ranks of spearmen and archers, above all the waggon train strung out along the road for almost twenty miles. An eye witness wrote, "All who were present agreed that never in our times has such an army gone forth from England." Despite the size of the army it made good speed, pausing only briefly for meals and allowing the minimum time for rest periods. The English host reached Edinburgh on 19th June and the following day moved to Falkirk—a remarkable feat for a force of this size to cover twenty miles in a single day. Barely a dozen miles away the Scottish host, in four columns, prepared to move out of Torwood. Robert himself commanded the Scottish rearguard, covering the eastern side of the Scottish position, Randolph commanded the vanguard on the side nearest to Stirling and the other two columns were under the respective command of Walter Stewart (son of the Steward and future progenitor of the Stewart dynasty) and Edward Bruce. James Douglas, who received the accolade on the eve of the battle, served under the youthful Stewart but was the real commander of that brigade.

On Saturday 22nd June, while the English army footslogged it to Falkirk, the Scots made a leisurely withdrawal from Torwood and took up their battle stations about a mile to the north in more open country, the lightly wooded New Park immediately north of the Bannock Burn, and here they waited for the English to approach. The main road, along which the English would be expected to go, ran almost due north and south from Torwood, down the incline to the Bannock Burn, across the Milton Bog and up the slope into the New Park near the Borestone. Half a mile to the east, where the burn ran through a deep gully to the open carse or marshland, was a clachan named Bannok, where the modern village of Bannockburn now stands. On the small plateau of cornfields north of the hamlet the battle is now thought to have been fought. It would seem obvious that the Battle of Bannockburn was actually fought at Bannockburn; but Professor Barrow was the first scholar to identify the site here and has argued cogently in its favour. The traditional site of the battle was in the New Park itself, where the Borestone and the Bruce equestrian statue stand. Miller (1931) and Carruthers (1933) located the main action a thousand yards to the east, at Dryfield of Balquhiderock, Mackay Mackenzie (1932—in rebuttal of Miller) placed the battle two miles from the Borestone, on the Carse of Stirling opposite Cambuskenneth Abbey, while General Christison (1959) identified the battleground as the Carse of Balquhiderock, near the confluence of the Bannock and Pelstream Burns. Much of this historic confusion has been caused by the assumption that the battle was named after the *stream* rather than after the *village,* and it is significant that the battle, if it had a name at all in contemporary circles, was known as the battle of Stirling, after the castle which was the main bone of contention.

On the morning of Sunday 23rd June the Scots army celebrated mass and breakfasted lightly on bread and water. The king's brigade was ranged near the Borestone, facing south across the Bannock Burn and guarding the road which seemed the likeliest approach for the English. There were several other alternatives, of course, and Robert had considered them carefully. The first was that the English might try to outflank him by approaching through the broken ground to the west of the New Park, so the woodland tracks on that side were barricaded with boulders. The second alternative—a movement east of the road—was unlikely since it would have exposed the English column to a flanking attack by the Scots from higher ground. There was a third alternative which Robert did not foresee, though his genius as a general is demonstrated by the way in which he faced this problem when it arose and turned it to his advantage. This line followed a footpath, running north from the village of Bannockburn, out of the gully of the burn and along the edge of the plateau of Balquhiderock to Stirling.

Sunday was a bright and sunny day, with conditions ideal for

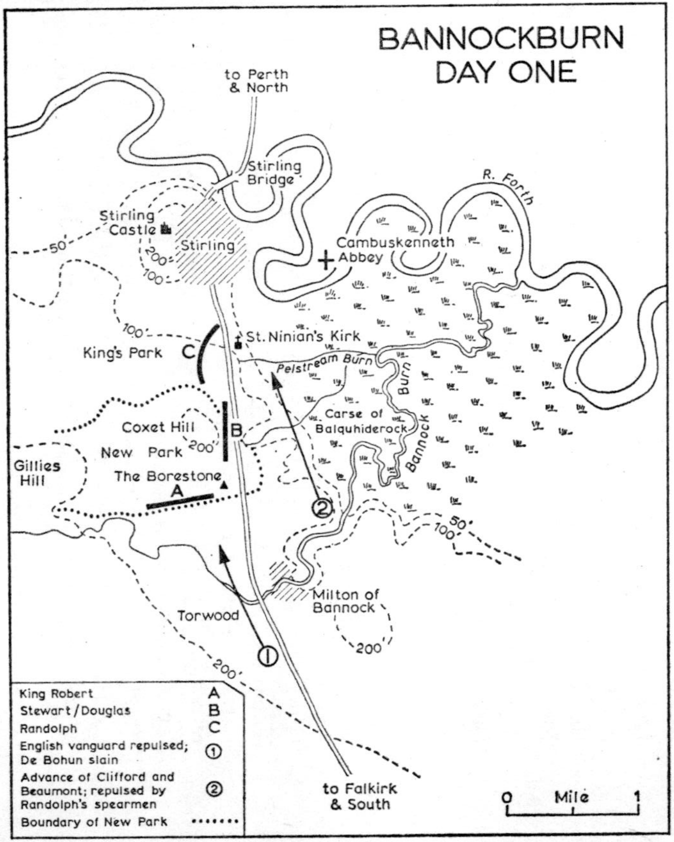
BANNOCKBURN
DAY ONE
to Perth & North
Stirling Bridge
Stirling Castle
Stirling
Cambuskenneth Abbey
R. Forth
50'
200'
100'
100'
King's Park
C
St. Ninian's Kirk
Pelstream Burn
Burn
Bannock
Carse of Balquhiderock
Coxet Hill
B
200'
New Park
Gillies Hill
The Borestone
A
2
50'
100'
Milton of Bannock
Torwood
1
200'
200'
to Falkirk & South
0 Mile 1
King Robert A
Stewart/Douglas B
Randolph C
English vanguard repulsed; De Bohun slain 1
Advance of Clifford and Beaumont; repulsed by Randolph's spearmen 2
Boundary of New Park

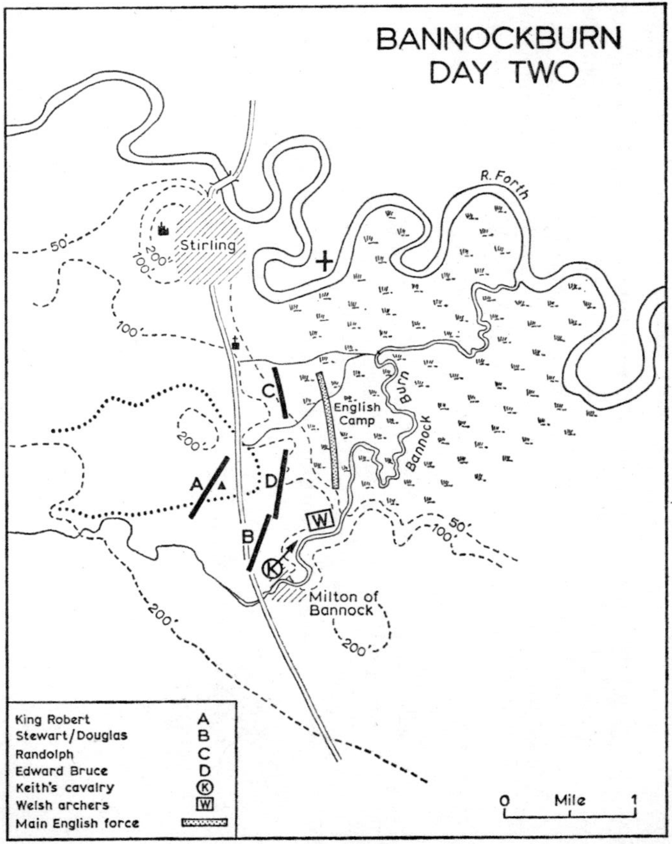
BANNOCKBURN
DAY TWO
R. Forth
Stirling
50'
200'
100'
100'
C
English Camp
Burn
Bannock
200'
A
D
W
50'
100'
B
K
Milton of Bannock
200'
200'
0 Mile 1
King Robert A
Stewart/Douglas B
Randolph C
Edward Bruce D
Keith's cavalry K
Welsh archers W
Main English force

a major battle according to the medieval rules of war. Bruce sent Douglas and Keith out on the road south to spy out the land. They were dismayed to see the colourful surcoats and gleaming lances of the English heavy cavalry advancing from Falkirk in their direction. They hurried back to give Robert the news. Perhaps he remembered the panic caused by Percy's cavalry at Irvine all those years before; at any rate he counselled Douglas and Keith to keep quiet about what they had seen, and carried on unperturbed.

The English cavalry with " banners, standards, pennants and spears " advanced through the woods to the south of Bannockburn, under the joint command of Edward's young nephew, Gilbert de Clare, Earl of Gloucester, and Humphrey de Bohun, Constable of England. There was a clash of personalities between these two men, lords of rival earldoms in the western marches. Edward's appointment of his nephew was regarded by the proud de Bohun as an affront. In the circumstances it was unlikely that quick decisions would be taken if the occasion demanded. A few miles south of the Scottish lines the English vanguard met Sir Philip de Moubray, the commander of Stirling Castle, who had ridden out to meet them. He may have had a safe conduct from the Scots, or he may have taken a circuitous route, far to the west of the New Park, to reach the English host, and thus would have warned the relieving force that the woodland tracks had been blocked and the park was strongly held by the Scots. In any event the English had fulfilled their part of the bargain made by Edward Bruce the previous summer; by coming so close to Stirling they had absolved Moubray from his obligation to surrender the castle. His advice, therefore, was probably to hold off in the hope that the Scottish army would withdraw quietly without a fight.

The English vanguard, however, was spoiling for a fight. Gloucester and Hereford led their men on and rode out of the Torwood. Ahead, on the far side of the depression and the Bannock Burn, they saw what they took to be a rabble of Scots retreating into the New Park. This was what they were waiting for. Recklessly they spurred their destriers forward, crossed the stream and charged blindly up the slope towards the Scots. In the forefront was young Henry de Bohun, the Earl of Hereford's nephew, eager to prove his knighthood that day. Before him he spotted a Scottish knight mounted on a pony and armed with a battle-axe. As de Bohun cantered up to the knight he realized jubilantly that this was none other than the king of Scots, identified by the coronet atop his helmet. De Bohun rode at Bruce, full tilt, but the king wheeled and let the heavily-armoured knight clatter past. With coolness and what must have been superb timing, King Robert rose in his stirrups as de Bohun passed him, and struck him a fearful blow with his axe, ripping into de Bohun's helmet and cleaving his skull from crown to chin. The luckless knight toppled from his charger and the king was left with the shattered haft of his axe. The Scots were electrified by this exhibition of axemanship. The officers berated their king for taking such a risk but he merely shrugged his shoulders and said that he was just sorry that he had broken such a good axe. News of this incident must have spread like wildfire through the Scottish ranks. With such a superman at their head, how could they fail. One can imagine the exultant mood in the Scottish army after de Bohun was thus brought low.

As for the rest of the English vanguard—there was a brisk encounter with the Scots. The English knights sustained considerable casualties and Gloucester, who was unseated at one point, was lucky to escape with his life. The English withdrew to the other bank of the burn with the Scots in hot pursuit and it was all that Robert could do to recall them before the situation got out of hand. The drama of de Bohun's death and the unexpected ferocity of the Scottish counter-attack sobered the English somewhat. A frontal attack along the road was clearly unwise so an alternative route had to be found. It was then that Clifford and Sir Henry Beaumont took the path northwards from the village, leading a force of cavalry variously estimated at 300 to 800, below the ridge of Balquhiderock. From this path the towers and battlements of Stirling Castle can be clearly discerned, barely two miles away across the low-lying carse, and it may have been the object of relieving the castle by the most direct route which impelled this squadron of knights to gallop northwards. This body of heavy cavalry moved forward in close order until they were level with St. Ninian's Kirk, where the Pelstream Burn cut across their line of advance. They had ridden perhaps half a mile without attracting the unwelcome attention of the Scots arrayed on the heights to the west in the New Park—but they had not reckoned with the eagle eye of King Robert who suddenly observed the movement of horses out on the carse.

Randolph's brigade had been assigned the task of guarding the road near St. Ninian's Kirk in case the English should break through the Scottish vanguard and try to outflank the main body of troops. Obviously Robert had not considered that the English would actually ride across the soft ground bordering the carse itself—but here they were. Randolph was actually conferring with the king as Clifford's men rode north. Robert turned to Randolph and observed drily that a rose had fallen from his chaplet. In modern times he might have said that a feather had slipped from his cap. Stung by this reproach, and angry with himself for having failed to check the English advance, Randolph galloped back up the road to his troops by the church and ordered his spearmen down the slope to the path to intercept the English cavalry. Randolph halted his infantry and formed them into the dreaded schiltrom, a veritable hedgehog of spears to block the enemy advance. According to Barbour, Beaumont said "Let them come on. Give them some ground. We must draw back a little." He realized that the cavalry would need room in which to manoeuvre. Sir Thomas Grey (father of the chronicler) retorted, "Give them what you like now; I'm afraid that soon they will have everything." Beaumont sneered at this and told him to run for it if he was so afraid. "Fear will not make me flee, my lord," replied Grey as he and Sir William Deyncourt urged their steeds forward into the bristling line of spears. Deyncourt was killed instantly; Grey's horse was killed under him and he was promptly captured.

The same fate, or worse, befell many an English knight in the ensuing mêlée. Randolph's spearmen were well trained and kept formation. The English knights lost their heads and charged and wheeled recklessly, trying by sheer bravado to break the ranks of spears. The Scots coolly bore this onslaught, killing the horses and unseating the heavily-armoured knights. Unhorsed, the latter were no match for the nimble spearmen. The lesson of Falkirk sixteen years earlier had been forgotten; then the schiltroms had been broken by the deadly fire of the

Cast of the skull of King Robert Bruce

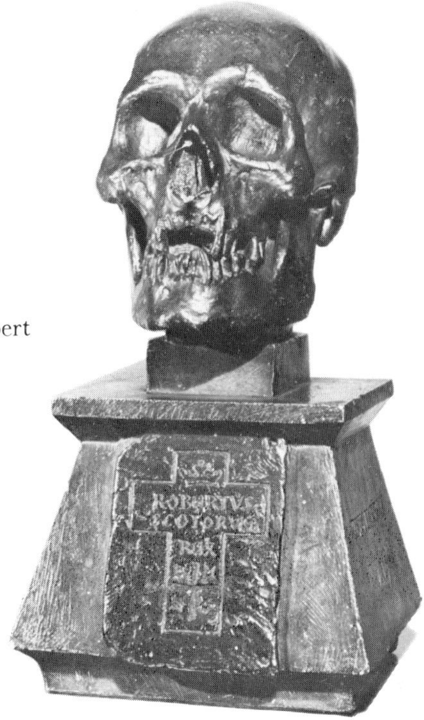

The silver penny of King Robert Bruce

The Great Seal of King Robert Bruce

Portrait of King Robert Bruce by de Witt at Holyrood

longbowmen before the cavalry finished the job, but now Clifford and Beaumont had ridden forward without infantry in support. At length the cavalry attack broke in confusion and the Scots drove them off with heavy losses. Ironically, what remained of the squadron fled to the doubtful shelter of Stirling Castle, though Clifford himself managed to get back to the main army. Douglas, impatient at the inaction of his troops while Randolph's men had all the sport, persuaded Robert to let him lead a squadron of cavalry to Randolph's assistance. But when Douglas's troopers rode out of the wood they saw that the spearmen were getting the better of the English and they politely held back. The mere sight of the Scottish reinforcements, however, may have been enough to make Clifford and Beaumont realize the hopelessness of their plight. The defeat of the English on what is known to this day as Randolph's Field was highly significant. It proved that the mobile schiltrom was effective against cavalry unsupported by archers. More immediately the rout of the English cavalry, at little cost in Scottish casualties, raised the Scots' morale even higher, with a correspondingly depressing effect on the English.

By the time the scattered remnants of Clifford's and Beaumont's force got back to the English lines it was too late in the day for a further attack. It is important to bear in mind that owing to the nature of the terrain the bulk of the English troops had not had a sight of the Scots as yet, far less actually got to grips with them, and the news of the two defeats inflicted already would have lost nothing in the telling. Footsore and weary and no doubt suffering the effects of the midsummer heat, the English host were not exactly in the best condition to tackle the Scots. Nightfall brought a welcome respite, though the fear that Bruce might stage a counter-attack after dark prevented the English from getting the sleep they needed. It was this fear that induced the English to make a fatal mistake. A safe place had to be found where they could bivouac for the night. Normally they might have paused where they were, but the general staff considered that the level ground on the carse, beyond the Bannock Burn, would be a better place, since there was plenty of water there for the horses—probably not far short of three thousand in all—which were now showing the ill-effects of the unseasonably hot weather. In the waggon train there were about a thousand oxen, and these beasts also needed water; and the men who had endured two forced marches along dusty roads were also badly in need of a good drink.

Consequently, under cover of darkness, the cavalry and the commissariat made the difficult crossing of the Bannock Burn, " an evil, deep and boggy stream " as Grey described it, and took up their positions on the carse. They had a great deal of trouble crossing the pows, or sluggish streams of the carse, and had to improvise bridges from the doors and beams of houses. Barbour says that the beleaguered garrison in Stirling Castle even sallied forth after midnight with materials to help the relieving army to cross these inconvenient streams. With this hectic activity and the task of cleaning weapons and equipment in preparation for the coming day, it can be imagined that the English troops got little sleep that night. The carse, after dark, was a cold, damp place and the soldiers had to resort to liquor to keep their spirits up and keep out the cold.

Meanwhile, unaware of the state of the English army, the Scots were actually thinking of evacuating their positions and retreating into the wilder, more remote parts of the country to avoid a pitched battle. Bruce was just contemplating such a withdrawal to the Lennox when a Scottish knight serving in the English army, named Sir Alexander Seton, rode into the Scottish camp. Judging from his name he may have been a relation of those Setons who had given their lives in Robert's service years before. Like Sir Richard Lundin at Irvine, Seton was disgusted at the panic and confusion in the English ranks and he decided that the time had come to desert. He brought to Robert the valuable intelligence that the English were in a demoralized state and that a golden opportunity had arisen for the Scots to defeat their enemy. Bruce considered this news and then consulted his staff. Should they fight or withdraw? They answered unanimously, " Good King, as soon as day comes tomorrow order yourself and your army for battle. We shall not fail for fear of death, nor flinch at any suffering till we have made our country free."

Chapter XI

The Longest Day

Dawn broke on Midsummer Day at 3.45 a.m. Down on the carse the English troops awoke from their uneasy slumbers, stretched their cramped limbs and peered westward where the first thin rays of the sun picked out the trees of the New Park where lay their adversaries. The Scots were up with the dawn, having rested well and in comparative comfort. The chaplains celebrated mass before the assembled multitude. The day was the feast-day of St. John the Baptist and the lesson was taken from the book of Isaiah, chapter 40: " Comfort ye, comfort ye, my people . . . Speak ye comfortably to Jerusalem, and cry unto her that her warfare is accomplished . . ." Then, as in so many later conflicts, the Scots drew inspiration from the Scriptures. Abbot Maurice of Inchaffray gave his benediction and then the king addressed the men.

> My lords, my people, accustomed to enjoy that full freedom for which in times gone by the kings of Scotland have fought many a battle! For eight years or more I have struggled with much labour for my right to the kingdom and for honourable liberty. I have lost brothers, friends and kinsmen. Your own kinsmen have been made captive, and bishops and priests are locked in prison. Our country's nobility has poured forth its blood in war. Those barons you can see before you, clad in mail, are bent upon destroying me and obliterating my kingdom, nay, our whole nation. They do not believe that we can survive. They glory in their warhorses and equipment. For us, the name of the Lord must be our hope of victory in battle. This day is a day of rejoicing: the birthday of John the Baptist. With Our Lord Jesus Christ as commander, Saint

Andrew and the martyr Saint Thomas shall fight with the saints of Scotland for the honour of their country and their nation. If you heartily repent of your sins you will be victorious, under God's command. As for offences committed against the Crown, I proclaim a pardon by virtue of my royal power, to all those who fight manfully for the kingdom of our fathers.

This stirring appeal to the innate religious fervour of the Scots had the desired effect. This was to be a day on which God was on the side of the small battalions for once. On a more practical note, however, Bruce also promised a general remission of all feudal death duties in respect of every man who might be killed in battle.

It was at this time that the accolade was bestowed on a number of knights, including young Walter Stewart and James Douglas. That Douglas received his knighthood only at this time, when he had held high rank in the Scottish army for so long, seems surprising, but Barbour's phrase, that they were made knights "ilk ane in their degree" seems to imply that Douglas may have been raised to a higher rank of knighthood, from a simple knight to a knight banneret.

Shortly after daybreak the English cavalry mounted up and moved out of the marshy carse. They advanced in extended line towards the south-west, up a fifty-foot slope on to the firm level ground of the Dryfield of Balquhiderock. Keeping his own brigade in reserve near the Borestone Robert sent forward the three other brigades under his brother Edward, Douglas and Randolph to meet the oncoming cavalry. The Scottish infantry, with supporting cavalry, marched out of the wood, their banners fluttering bravely in the morning sunlight. Edward Bruce's brigade led the way, with Randolph's brigade on his left, slightly to the rear, and Douglas's brigade to the rear of his right flank. When they were clear of the wood the Scottish schiltroms halted and formed up in full view of the enemy. The Scots knelt and recited the Lord's Prayer, commending their souls to God's care.

It must have been a moving sight. To King Edward, who was astonished that the Scots should dare to offer battle at all, it seemed incredible and he misinterpreted it. Commenting to his staff he said, "These men kneel to beg for mercy." According to Barbour Sir Ingelram de Umfraville retorted (as one who should have known), "You are right. They ask for mercy, but not from you. They seek it from God, for their sins."

The Earl of Gloucester had advised Edward to postpone the battle for a day, to give the men time to recover. According to Barbour, Umfraville even suggested to the king that they should feign a retreat beyond their baggage lines, to tempt the Scots into the carse where the cavalry could slaughter them. But such advice is both unlikely and unwise. Edward realized that, having led his troops into a difficult situation, he had no alternative but face the Scots and make the best of it. The English host pressed forward up the slope on to the hard ground, realizing too late that they had no room to manoeuvre. The vanguard halted, but the rearguard continued to press on and soon the English cavalry was a dense, confused mass. Someone had the sense to post the Welsh archers along the northern side of the gully of the Bannock Burn, where they could shoot at the Scottish schiltroms. With memories of the battle of Falkirk, Bruce quickly mustered his own bowmen to deal with this menace, and sent the Marischal and his cavalry to ride down the enemy archers. Keith's squadron was concealed in dead ground almost until they were on top of the archers and the impact of their charge drove the unfortunate Welshmen into the ravine with heavy losses.

The English vanguard continued to struggle forward. Some say that Gloucester and Hereford quarelled again over who should take the lead. Gloucester spurred his mount ahead of his troops, and was promptly skewered by the Scottish spearmen. In vain did the rest of his brigade charge after him. The heavily-armoured knights failed to dent the impenetrable forest of spears. The flower of English chivalry was hurled against the Scots, and perished on the points of those determined spears. Among the dead in this initial onslaught were Sir Robert Clifford and Sir John Comyn, whose father Robert Bruce had stabbed eight years previously.

The vanguard reeled before the schiltrom of Edward Bruce, and fell back in confusion against the remaining brigades, now tightly packed in the narrow strip of level ground. Now the other Scottish brigades, led by Randolph and Douglas, advanced and levelled their spears at the milling horses. Barbour gives a graphic account of this engagement, describing the ring of spear-point on helmet and mail, the screams of the disembowelled horses, the grass reddened by the blood of men and animals. With the elimination of the English archers the Scots were more than a match for the English cavalry. The schiltrom had been proved effective against cavalry at Courtrai in 1302 and it was to demonstrate its deadliness at Morgarten the following year. Now all three Scottish brigades were in action, in line abreast across the front of the level ground, and pressing steadily forward against the confused tangle of enemy horse.

Again we see Robert's superb sense of timing. At the right moment he brought up his own brigade on the right of the Scottish line and hurled his own troops into the mêlée. The English gave ground before this mad onrush, and trampled each other underfoot. The Scots dourly jabbed their way forward into the mass of English cavalry. The Scots were exultant; the English were desperate. They were being gradually forced down the incline, with the dangerous gorge of the Bannock Burn on their left and the treacherous marshes and streams of the carse behind them. Beyond lay the meandering Forth, too deep and too wide for anyone to get across to safety. It was the same situation that had faced the English at the battle of Stirling Bridge in 1297, and once more the loops of the Forth were ensnaring the English cavalry.

The battle was definitely going in the Scottish favour when the English perceived what they took to be yet another brigade marching on to the field. These were the 'camp followers', the lightly armed rabble of clerks, orderlies, labourers and general duty men who are indispensable in every well-run army but are seldom involved in the actual fighting. These men had been left behind in the New Park with the waggons and baggage, perhaps at Gillies Hill thus named in their honour. King Robert can hardly have welcomed this undisciplined nob, probably intent on plundering the corpses; the battlefield was already overcrowded as it was. But the hard-pressed English were in no position to discriminate between fresh combat troops and camp followers. They turned and fled as best they could. The irony is that although all four brigades of the Scottish army were now engaged, few—if any—of the English infantry had even crossed the Bannock Burn, far less got themselves involved in the fighting. Yet the English infantry alone numbered twice that of the entire Scottish army, even at a conservative estimate.

The veteran Earl of Pembroke realized the danger if the king were captured. Such a calamity would have a disastrous effect not only on England's future ability to overcome Scotland, but also on England's status among the European powers. With his squadron of knights he hustled the king, protesting, from the battlefield and escorted him along the path towards Stirling on the edge of the carse. This dishonourable retreat was more than one illustrious knight could stomach. Sir Giles d'Argentan was reputed to be the third finest knight in Christendom.* Not long before, he had had the misfortune to end up in a Byzantine jail, but Edward had personally written to the Empress at Constantinople to secure his release. Now Sir Giles left the king's bodyguard and rode back into the fray, hurling himself to certain death on the spears of the leading schiltrom.

It would have taken much more than the self-sacrifice of Sir Giles to avert disaster. When the English realized that their lord and master had fled the field they turned in blind panic. The retreat turned quickly into headlong flight. Many were drowned in the " evil, deep and boggy stream "; others floundered in the pows or were swept away in the Forth itself. The press of drowned corpses in the Bannock Burn was so tight that " Men mycht pass dry atour it then ", as Barbour put it laconically. The battle was aptly named, for it was in the Bannock Burn that disaster overtook the fleeing English. As the cavalry stampeded back towards the gully they plunged over on top of each other, so that many were crushed rather than drowned. At all events it was a horrible end to the débâcle.

The English infantry made good its escape, relatively unharmed; but the principal teeth arm, the cavalry, suffered grievously. The death roll would have read like an early edition of Debrett: one earl and almost forty barons alone were killed on the English side at Bannockburn. Gloucester was that Gilbert de Clare, grand-nephew of the Competitor Bruce and therefore a cousin of King Robert. The king had his body taken from the battlefield and laid in state in a nearby church where the king himself kept an all-night vigil. The corpses of the Earl of

* The finest Knights at that time were reputed to be Robert Bruce and Henry of Luxembourg – in that order.

Gloucester and Sir Robert de Clifford were subsequently handed over to King Edward.

Moubray, who had apparently fought in the English ranks that day and had witnessed the slaughter, rode back as fast as he could to the relative safety of Stirling Castle. Shortly afterwards King Edward and the Earl of Pembroke arrived at the castle gates and demanded to be let in. The accounts of this incident vary. One version is that Moubray told the king that he could come in if he wished, but by the terms of the agreement with Edward Bruce the castle would have to be surrendered to the Scots. Another version is less kind; Moubray raised the drawbridge and told his erstwhile master to be off. The royal party made off again, making a wide detour round Gillies Hill to avoid the victorious Scots, and headed east towards Dunbar. The presence of a large and comparatively orderly body of cavalry could not go long undetected in the aftermath of Bannockburn and news of the king's whereabouts soon reached Douglas who had been instructed to take a troop of sixty horse and hunt down stragglers from Edward's retinue. Douglas and his men shadowed Edward all the way to Lothian, harrying them incessantly so that, as Barbour puts it, " they had not even time to make water ". It was a greatly reduced party which eventually reached the safety of Dunbar Castle. Earl Patrick received Edward and Pembroke as best he could and saw his royal visitor safely aboard a ship which took the Plantagenet to Bamburgh and thence back to Berwick. The bulk of his bodyguard, however, had to fend for themselves and make the journey to Berwick overland. On his return to England Edward founded Oriel College, Oxford as a thanksgiving—the only positive thing that England gained as a result of that sorry campaign. Incidentally the tombstone of a Provost of Oriel now adorns the belfry of St. Ninian's Kirk.

Meanwhile Stirling Castle, whose relief had been the cause of the campaign, continued to hold out. Its garrison was greatly augmented by refugees from the battlefield who scaled the castle rock and tried to defend themselves as best they could. Robert was obliged to detach a sizeable portion of his army to attack the castle and round up its defenders. Most of the English fled southwards and made for Carlisle. A large party of cavalry under the Earl of Hereford, however, took refuge in Bothwell

Castle which still held out against the Scots. Its constable, a Scot, decided that the time had come to change sides and promptly turned over his guests to the Scots. This was a rich prize indeed, since the Earl's party included John de Segrave and the Umfraville brothers, Ingelram and Robert, Earl of Angus. They were eventually released on payment of a stiff ransom. For the Earl of Hereford, King Robert secured the release of the ladies of his family as well as Bishop Wishart, now old and blind. On the whole Robert dealt kindly with his prisoners, as befitted such a " parfait gentil knight ". He was able to repay the good deed of Ralph de Monthermer (who had tipped him off in 1305–6 that Comyn had betrayed him to Edward) and released him after Bannockburn free of ransom. The Walsingham chronicler Trokelowe, grudgingly admitted that Robert behaved chivalrously towards his discomfited enemies so that he completely won their hearts. Regrettably, but understandably, this humane and courteous conduct did not always extend downwards through the ranks. Many of the English rank and file whose families would not be able to raise a ransom for their release were butchered after the battle, and woe betide the straggler luckless enough to fall into the hands of the Scottish peasantry who combed the countryside for weeks afterwards seeking Englishmen on whom to wreak vengeance for the years of harsh, foreign rule.

The Earl of Pembroke, having left the king's side, organized one of the least-known deeds of the campaign which ought to rank with Sir John Moore's withdrawal at Corunna or the evacuation of Dunkirk in 1940. The Welsh levies were left to fend for themselves, ill-equipped, half-clothed in a strange land whose tongue they did not understand. Aymer de Valence, whose earldom lay in their territory, succoured this enormous band of stragglers, perhaps running into thousands, and skilfully guided them through hostile territory to Carlisle. Though the Scots harried and slaughtered the stragglers unmercifully the bulk of the Welsh contingent crossed the Solway intact, thanks to the resourcefulness and bravery of their leader. Having escaped the clutches of the Scots, Pembroke had the misfortune later to be captured by a Burgundian while on his way to Rome. He was taken into custody in Imperial territory and a ransom of £20,000 had to be paid to win him his freedom.

One of the more bizarre prisoners taken by the Scots was the clerk Baston, employed by Edward in some sort of position which nowadays would come under the heading of 'public relations'. Like many a journalist, before and since, Baston wrote an account of the campaign, in verse, before the event and accompanied the expedition merely to fill in some of the local colour. Baston's epic poem caused no end of hilarity to the Scots who insisted, however, that he make the necessary alterations to his glowing account of the great victory before they let him go. Baston was obviously a good journalist, able to write a story from either viewpoint, and promptly obliged his captors, transposing the names of Edward and Robert where applicable.

In monetary terms the victory of Bannockburn was considerable. The Scots captured the much-vaunted, long strung-out English baggage train intact and its contents (which included gold plate and costly silks) were estimated at £200,000—an astronomical sum if related to current money values. Almost 500 noble prisoners were subsequently released on payment of suitable ransoms. But the true value of this victory cannot be measured in cash. The defeat of the English was decisive in the sense that Scotland was at last cleared of foreign troops (only Berwick remained in English hands) and the country was now united as never before behind King Robert. Of course there are many imponderables about this campaign. If the Scots had had sufficient cavalry to press home their victory, if Edward had been killed or captured, the history of Anglo-Scottish relations might have turned out differently. The war was to last a further fourteen years and occupy all but a few short months of Robert's reign. But though the war was to drag on wearily it was effectively won that summer's day at Bannockburn. Scotland was independent and Bruce was her king—though the English took a long time to recognize these accomplished facts.

Chapter XII

Alarums and Excursions

In July 1314, with Scotland united behind Robert and the English on the run, peace seemed to be in sight. Robert waited for several weeks, confident that peace overtures would now be made by the English court, but none came. Instead of adopting a sensible view of the situation and acceding to Robert's not unreasonable demands for recognition, Edward was smarting under the blow—the most resounding defeat ever suffered by an English army—and was doubtless motivated by the desire for revenge though he was hardly in a position to implement his feelings. Back home in London he had a different perspective on the affair. Scotland and Bannockburn seemed very remote to those at Westminster and in time it was more comforting to look back on the campaign as no more than a stroke of ill-luck and not a true indication of Scottish prowess or determination to be rid of English rule. It has been argued that if a pitched battle had been avoided there would have been no dramatic show-down. Edward's progress through Scotland would have fizzled out as his previous campaign had done and this would have led to a succession of truces which would inevitably have developed into lasting peace once the heat was taken out of the situation. On the other hand, the time had to come when Robert was prepared to take a stand against the English. Guerrilla tactics were all very well but even that kind of war needs its decisive battles and signal successes if morale is to be maintained.

There was a new mood in Scotland after Bannockburn. Lothian was cleared of the English and only the extreme south-eastern tip of the country, round Berwick, remained in English hands. The barons and knights who had served Edward now defected to Robert and served him and Scotland with unswerving loyalty. Edward and his advisers failed to realize the new mood of solidarity in Scotland or the aggressive spirit of its people. Victory over a supposedly master race had an almost intoxicating effect on the Scots and this is reflected in the ensuing campaigns. From 1314 onwards the war was taken into the enemy camp; Henceforward there was to be very little fighting in Scotland itself. If Edward was too pig-headed to acknowledge Scottish independence he must be taught a lesson by force. At the beginning of August, therefore, Robert sent his brother and Douglas with a strong body of men raiding deep into north-eastern England. They systematically ravaged Northumberland, County Durham and Teesdale, seizing vast quantities of booty, taking large sums of money in blackmail and terrorizing the inhabitants. Subsequently Robert wrote to Edward suggesting peace terms and appointing as commissioners the Constable, Sir Gilbert Hay, the Marischal, Sir Robert Keith, Neil Campbell and Roger Kirkpatrick. Edward convened a parliament at York to discuss the Scottish terms and later sent commissioners to treat with the Scots at Dumfries. The English were quite willing to have a truce, but the appointment of the Earl of Pembroke as Guardian of England north of the Trent seemed an ominous move. In the end the negotiations broke down because the English refused to recognize Robert as king or to waive their claim to suzerainty.

In November Robert convened a parliament at Cambuskenneth, the principal business of which was the problem of those landowners who had opposed the king and had not yet come into his peace. Robert showed great wisdom in his handling of this situation. He was resolutely opposed to forfeiture and a year's grace was given to those who still held allegiance to the English king before they would be dispossessed. Many noblemen came over to Robert in the immediate aftermath of Bannockburn but most of the others made their peace with him and swore fealty to him in the ensuing months. A notable exception to this was David, Earl of Atholl, son-in-law of the murdered Comyn and a consistent supporter of King Edward until 1312 when he changed sides. At that time Robert confirmed him in the office of Constable and restored his earldom. The Earl of Atholl later took a prominent part in the capture of Perth in 1313, but his allegiance to the Bruce cause was soured by the waywardness of Edward Bruce who, having married Earl David's sister Isabel, then abandoned her in favour of the sister of Sir Walter de Ross. On the very eve of Bannockburn the Earl of Atholl switched sides once more, treacherously attacking the Scottish supply depot at Cambuskenneth Abbey, killing the garrison and making off with the rations intended for the Scottish army. Sir Walter de Ross, himself, was killed in the battle, much to the grief of Sir Edward Bruce, and his erstwhile brother-in-law's treachery greatly embittered him. King Robert dispossessed Earl David, granting his earldom and lands to Neil Campbell of Lochawe, who married Mary Bruce after her release from English captivity. His office of Constable was given to Sir Gilbert Hay whose family, the earls of Errol, have held it ever since.

In the depths of winter the Scots raided England again, choosing Cumberland this time. The gentry of that district scraped together a handsome sum of money, with which they bought a respite from Scottish depradations until Midsummer 1315. In April 1315 parliament met again, this time at Ayr. Appropriately the main topic for discussion centred on King Robert himself. Robert was now turned forty and no doubt worried about securing the throne for his heirs and successors, in the interest of the maintenance of strong and settled government. Now that he was re-united with his wife there were hopes that she would produce a son—though almost a decade elapsed before this wish was granted. In the meantime the succession had to be clearly defined. Robert's daughter Marjorie, by his first wife, was now about twenty years old and betrothed to Walter Stewart, but with the continuance of the struggle against England it was imperative that a responsibility for the administration should devolve on a king rather than a queen. Marjorie herself agreed to waive her rights, in favour of the king's brother, described in the enabling act as " a man both strenuous and experienced in the arts of war for the defence of the liberties and laws of the Kingdom of Scotland ". Edward was now created Earl of Carrick and officially designated as Robert's successor. His heirs male were to follow, then Marjorie and her heirs. In the event of the succession of a minor, Thomas

Randolph, now Earl of Moray, was to act as regent.

The campaigning in 1315 followed the pattern set in the autumn and winter of the previous year. Sir James Douglas and the Earl of Moray led an expedition to County Durham and devastated it. These raids bore little resemblance to the haphazard, ill-disciplined incursions of Balliol's time, but were conducted systematically with the objects of securing food supplies (on the hoof), and cash in the form of ransom or blackmail, and terrorizing the English. These expeditions, at regular intervals, became part of the way of life of northern England for a decade, by the end of which the country north of the Humber and Trent was totally impoverished and largely denuded of population. The raiders were known as hobelars, from the sturdy ponies (hobins) which gave them such extraordinary mobility. They lived rough and ate little. Each man carried a bag of oatmeal and a girdle, or iron plate, on which to bake the bannocks which formed their staple diet. They ranged far and wide, and the six northern counties of England was the field in which they reaped a fine harvest year after year. The Westminster government more or less abandoned the northern shires to their fate.

In the more orthodox forms of warfare, however, the Scots were not quite so successful. On 22nd July 1315 King Robert laid siege to Carlisle Castle which his farther had once governed. The Lanercost Chronicle describes in some detail the conduct of the siege. The Scots were hampered by the lack of equipment necessary for an assault on such a strongly-defended place. The garrison heavily outnumbered the attackers in artillery. Having failed to breach the walls with their one siege engine, the Scots tried to undermine the fortifications by driving tunnels or saps under the foundations. Next they trundled a siege tower, or belfrey, up to the walls for an assault on the ramparts, but the cumbersome machine sank up to the axles in the soft ground. Finally the Scots tried the same diversionary tactics which had been so successful at the capture of Edinburgh Castle, but this time the English were too wary for them and the attack was repulsed. After ten days the Scots withdrew in some confusion, hotly pursued by the defenders under Sir Andrew Harcla who inflicted heavy losses and captured the Scottish siege equipment. A grateful Edward later awarded a bounty of 1000 marks to the gallant Sir Andrew for his services on this occasion.

In January 1316 Robert and Douglas laid siege to Berwick, the last stronghold of Scotland in English hands. They staged a combined land and sea attack by night, but the moon appeared at the wrong moment and showed their positions to the watchful garrison and the attack was beaten off. The Scots then settled down to a more leisurely investment, cutting off supplies to the town and castle from the sea. In February the garrison mutinied on account of hunger, so a troop of Gascon knights was sent out of the castle to forage in the countryside. Sir James Douglas got wind of this raid and set off to intercept them. There was a sharp encouter near Coldstream—Douglas reckoned this was the fiercest skirmish he ever took part in—and most of the raiders were killed. The Anglo-Gascon party are said to have adopted a defensive schiltrom formation to beat off Douglas's horsemen, but it availed them not. In two subsequent engagements Douglas routed English raiders at Lintalee, near Jedburgh and in the vicinity of Berwick. Robert Neville of Raby, the Peacock of the North, was slain in the latter encounter. During the summer of 1316 the Scots resumed the offensive, raiding the north riding of Yorkshire and also penetrating the Furness district of Lancashire where their booty included large quantities of iron ore—a commodity which Scotland lacked at that time.

The year after Bannockburn saw the Scots embarking on a foreign adventure—the only digression which Robert permitted himself. The close relationship of the Scots and the Irish of Ulster has already been mentioned. In the aftermath of Bannockburn, however, the Scots took steps to strengthen this connection. Had it been successful it seems probable that the history of Ireland, down to the present day, might have taken a different course. Indeed, the history of England with regard to the Continent would also have been vastly different, for the better of all concerned.

In the winter of 1314–15 the O'Neills of Ulster apparently decided to make a bid for independence, emulating the Scots. They sent emissaries to Scotland seeking help and offering the throne of Ireland to Edward Bruce. Edward had no aversion to this and his brother could see the material advantages of securing a friendly Ireland as a counterpoise to England and a potential base for future operations against Wales and the west of England. Consequently Edward Bruce and the Earl of Moray set out from Ayr in May 1315 and crossed to Larne in Ulster with a small but highly trained expeditionary force. It is interesting to note that the officers in this expedition included Sir Philip Moubray, lately King Edward's constable of Stirling Castle. On 26th May the Scots landed at Carrickfergus, and promptly defeated the Anglo-Irish barons of Ulster. They made a truce with the defenders of Carrickfergus Castle and advanced south as far as Dundalk, then swung round and made for Connor in Antrim, where they defeated the Earl of Ulster, brother of Queen Elizabeth, in September. The Scots again headed south, defeated Roger Mortimer at Kenliss about the end of December and early in the new year routed the forces of Edmund Butler, Justiciar of Ireland, at Arscoll. In May 1316 Edward Bruce was crowned King of Ireland at Dundalk and then settled down to besiege Carrickfergus which had been left in the rear. Another truce was arranged, but a relieving force under Lord de Mandeville broke the truce and there was a sharp skirmish in which de Mandeville was killed and his troops routed. Carrickfergus was forced to capitulate in September.

Edward Bruce and Moray then returned to Scotland to report to King Robert and enlist his aid. Robert crossed over to Ireland in the late autumn with a considerable army, intending to subdue Ireland on his brother's behalf, and leaving Douglas and Walter Stewart as his regents. The winter campaign of 1316–17, however, was doomed to failure. Very little is known of this episode, and it is treated only cursorily in the chronicles and subsequent histories. Robert apparently encountered his old enemy, Bisset of the Glens of Antrim, and suffered a defeat at his hands, but the results must have been inconclusive. The campaign of the Bruce kings dragged on throughout the winter. In the spring they advanced on Louth, on the south-eastern borders of Ulster, and attempted to take Dublin but it was too formidable an obstacle so they by-passed it and marched across country, through Leinster and Munster as far as Limerick. There the Scottish progress ground to a halt, their lines of communication dangerously over-extended. This was a year of great hunger and epidemics—Ireland's history seems to have had more than its share—and these natural disasters, rather than feats of arms, drove the Scots into retreat. The retreat across Ireland was slow and arduous and it says much for King Robert's generalship that, like Pembroke and his Welshmen after Bannockburn, the Scots managed to get back to Ulster in one piece. Little is recorded of this long march, other than ugly tales of cannibalism among the native Irish. One little anecdote sheds light on Robert's character. The Scots were about to abandon a particularly dangerous position when the king learned that a camp-woman was in labour. Since the poor wretch was in no state to be moved, Robert held up the retreat rather than abandon the woman to the enemy. This act was hardly expedient, but it shows the compassion of the man, and that his reputation as the finest knight in Christendom was not solely based on military prowess.

The Scots failed to win over the southern Irish and fell back before a powerful force of English troops led by Edmund Butler and Richard de Clare based on Kilkenny in Leinster. It is not recorded whether the English attempted to do battle with the Scots, but the Bruces considered it more prudent to get back to the comparative safety of Ulster. The Irish expedition had turned out to be an expensive and unproductive digression and in March 1317 Robert returned to Scotland where more important matters clamoured for his attention. King Edward had decided that the time had come to teach the Scottish marauders a lesson and he called out the English host to muster at Lancaster. On account of innumerable hitches the assembly did not take place until October, which was rather late in the campaigning season. Edward quarrelled with his cousin, the Earl of Lancaster over the command of the troops and in the end the soldiers were stood down and then sent home. Rather more alarming, however, was the seaborne invasion of Fife by a Yorkshire contingent which landed near Inverkeithing and put the Sheriff and Earl of Fife to flight. Five miles inland, at Auchtertool, the fugitives were halted by William Sinclair, the fighting bishop of Dunkeld. He rebuked them for their cowardly behaviour and rode off, armed to the teeth, to do battle with the invaders himself. His rebuke stiffened the Scottish will to resist; the Fifers turned about and followed the bishop back to the coast where they dispersed the Yorkshiremen after a brisk fight in which many were killed and others drowned. The rest got back to their ships, weighed anchor and made the most of a fair wind. Sinclair's conduct so pleased the king that ever afterwards Robert always referred to him as his very own bishop. In July the Earl of Moray partially redeemed the failure of the Irish campaign by recapturing the Isle of Man, which remained in Scottish hands until 1333. Scottish activity in the Irish Sea was due mainly to Thomas Dun who commanded the privateers raiding English shipping and transporting supplies and provisions to the army of Edward Bruce. That Dun was a thorn in the flesh of the English maritime interests is borne out by the inordinate preparations in the summer of 1317 to build and equip a powerful warship with the sole object of tracking him down and putting him out of action. Despite this Dun continued to harry English shipping and even carried out a raid on the coast of Anglesey in conjunction with the Earl of Moray.

The year 1318 began well enough for the Scots. Peter Spalding, a citizen of Berwick said to be related to Sir Robert Keith, decided to defect to the Scots and offered to betray the section of the city wall under his command. News of this was brought to King Robert who decided that the risk of double-dealing was worth taking, and gave the necessary orders to Douglas and Moray. On the night of 1st–2nd April an assault force led by Sir James Douglas scaled the wall of Berwick at the appointed place and gained entry to the town without opposition. Thereafter the alarm was raised, there was a great deal of confused fighting, and the town itself was in Scottish hands, though the castle continued to hold out for a further eleven weeks before its garrison was starved into submission. Shortly afterwards three English castles—Harbottle, Mitford and Wark in Northumberland—fell to the Scots who pressed home their advantage by raiding Yorkshire on a large scale. They sacked Northallerton, Boroughbridge and Knaresborough and only spared Ripon from the flames on promise of a payment of a thousand marks. Six prominent burgesses were taken as hostages for the payment and when, more than two years later, the bulk of the debt was still outstanding, the wives of the hostages petitioned King Edward, asking that he should compel the citizenry of Ripon to pay up and so secure their husbands' release.

Two events occurred which brought personal tragedy to the Bruce family and imperilled the succession. In March 1316 Princess Marjorie, heavily *enceinte,* was thrown from her horse and killed. With commendable presence of mind surgeons were summoned and promptly cut open her abdomen, delivering a son from her dead body. The circumstances of his birth left their mark on the boy who was a cripple to the end of his days. As Robert II he ascended the throne in February 1370 (Old Style), the first and least auspicious of the ill-starred Stewarts. In 1318 Isobel of Atholl, the rejected wife of Edward Bruce, died and he was free at last to marry his mistress, Isobel de Ross. She had already borne him two children but since they had been borne out of wedlock they were regarded as illegitimate. Before the new Countess of Carrick could bear her lord a son and heir he was killed in battle at Dundalk in October. The deaths of Marjorie and her Uncle Edward triggered off a crisis; in December parliament met at Scone and passed a new Act of Succession, settling the crown on the king's infant grandson Robert. The tragic situation of thirty years earlier now seemed set for repetition. The Earl of Moray, grandson of the king's mother by her first marriage to Adam de Kilconquhar, was nominated regent in the event of King Robert's death. The earldom of Carrick reverted to the king and was conferred by him on his son David the year before his death. Later it was transferred by Regent Moray to Alexander Bruce, the elder child of Edward's liaison with Isobel de Ross.

Significantly this parliament achieved a great deal of work in other fields as well, primarily concerning the relationship between the church and the state. Shortly after Bannockburn Pope Clement had died, but there was such a dispute over his successor that it was not until 1316 that John XXII was appointed to fill the vacancy. Pope John, like his predecessor, was a Frenchman from Guyenne, a district which owed fealty to the king of England. Apart from his natural allegiance to Edward, the new pope regarded King Robert quite frankly as a troublemaker who was preventing the English from taking their rightful place in his pet project—a crusade against the infidel in the Holy Land. One of his first acts was to issue a bull,

Vocatis nobis, addressed to both Edward II and Robert, urging on them a truce. Rather tactlessly Edward's copy was addressed to him as " Our dearest son in Christ, Edward, illustrious King of England " whereas Robert's copy styled him as " Our dear son the noble Robert Bruce, acting as King of Scots ". When the Pope sent the Bishop of Corban and the Archdeacon of Perpignan to the Scottish court in September 1316 with the papal bull, Robert treated them courteously enough but refused to accept the document on the grounds that there were several gentlemen by the name of Robert Bruce and good manners forbade him from opening letters which might be intended for someone else! The envoys were forced to return to the Papal Legates, Cardinals Guacchini and Luca, without having secured Robert's assent to the proposed truce. The Legates tried again. This time they sent the Superior of the Franciscans at Berwick to intercede with Robert. The king asked him if he had a message for the King of Scots and when the embarrassed Franciscan said that his master did not (or could not) recognize such a person, Robert blandly refused to have anything further to do with him. To make matters worse the wretched cleric was waylaid on the return journey, stripped of his clothes and robbed of his papers, including the papal bull.

These were but light-hearted diversions. There were more serious aspects of the matter to be thrashed out. Bishop Wishart, repatriated after Bannockburn, died on 26th November 1316. During Wishart's imprisonment the organization of the diocese of Glasgow was largely in the hands of Robert's chancellor, Bernard of Linton and his chamberlain, Stephen of Dunnideer. After Wishart's death King Robert attempted to secure the election of Dunnideer to the see, but Edward II persuaded the Pope to veto this proposal. Dunnideer went to the Continent to get this decision changed, but died at Paris en route. Meanwhile Edward II secured the election of John of Egglescliffe, an English friar, but he never actually took office and seven years later he became Bishop of Llandaff. Robert next sought the election of John Lindsay and for the next few years he was *de facto* bishop, though he was not consecrated until 1323 when there was a rapprochement between Robert and Pope John.

Bishop Lamberton, imprisoned at the same time as Wishart,

was released in 1308 on condition that he remained in the diocese of Durham. He set up his headquarters at the northern extremity of the diocese, on the Scottish border, and for several years acted as a kind of mediator between Edward II and Robert, enjoying the confidence of both. He took an important part in all the truce negotiations up to 1312 when he went over to the Scots. Thereafter he continued to serve King Robert in both spiritual and temporal capacities. In July 1318 he officiated at the dedication of the cathedral of St. Andrews which had taken more than 150 years to build. The following year Edward tried hard to have Lamberton ejected from his see but failed. Thereafter English interference in the affairs of the Scottish church decreased considerably, and disappeared altogether after the papal reconciliation with the Scots in 1323.

The Scone parliament of December 1318 passed several acts for " the honour of God and Holy Mother Church, the amending of the land and the defence of the people." But apart from the statutes for the protection of the church, important ordinances established equality of all men before the law. Others laid down legal procedure and there were also regulations for the control of the fishing industry and for the conduct of the armed forces. One act forbade the export of money or goods from Scotland—a temporary measure aimed at those members of the nobility who were still sitting on the fence and had not decided whether to stay in Scotland or to transfer their Scottish property to their English or Continental estates. This act effectively eliminated the old international military caste of Anglo-Norman-French nobles, at least so far as Scotland was concerned. Robert himself had lost his English estates in 1306, and the men who followed him after that date, or came over to his side, were dispossessed of their estates in England. A generation elapsed before normal relations were resumed between Scotland and England, and by that time the ruling classes of Scotland had emerged in a distinctive form, with only tenuous links south of the Border.

Early in 1319 Edward decided to have one more attempt at the subjugation of the Scots. The memory of Bannockburn was strong, but only in the sense that Edward nursed a bitter sense of grievance and had a burning desire for revenge. He failed to learn anything from his defeat, however, and after five years of relative inaction felt that the time had come to put the rebellious Scots in their place. He patched up his quarrel with Thomas of Lancaster again and between them they mustered a host estimated at 8,000–12,000 men. Pope John sent Edward the sum of £2,500 from the Crusading Fund—hardly a tactful gesture. The English commanders included the veteran Pembroke, back from European captivity, and the Umfraville brothers, the last of the Balliol-Comyn faction to remain hostile to Robert. A combined land and sea force attacked Berwick on 7th September but the town was resoutely defended by Walter Stewart and the invaders repulsed after fierce fighting which lasted a week. Robert sent Douglas and Moray with their light cavalry to relieve the town. Instead of making a frontal attack on Edward's entrenched positions, the Scottish flying column bypassed Berwick and struck deep into Yorkshire, aiming for York itself where Edward's queen Isabelle was residing. Archbishop Melton had the royal party evacuated to Nottingham for safety and then rallied the citizens and clergy of York to meet the advancing Scots. This motley rabble of artisans, monks and priests intercepted the Scots at Myton, some twelve miles from York, where the Swale joins the Ouse. The experienced hobelars made short work of the archbishop's scratch force. The resulting massacre is known as the Chapter of Myton, an allusion to the great proportion of clergymen who fought and died that day. The archbishop, who subscribed to the view that any fool can be uncomfortable on the march, encumbered himself with a vast amount of expensive bedding, silver plate and other costly equipment—all of which had to be abandoned to the Scots.

This raid had the desired effect. The mere rumour of the Scots was enough to have everyone in the north of England bleating for protection and Edward was forced to raise the siege of Berwick and bring his troops back from the Scottish border. The campaign, so far as the English were concerned, had achieved nothing. The Scots, on the other hand, demonstrated yet again that they could raid England with impunity, and as if to emphasize this Douglas perpetrated his most brutal attack on England, raiding Gilsland and Westmorland at the end of October, just when the harvest was about to be gathered in, and destroying all the standing crops he could find. Edward realized that further action would be futile. He dispersed his troops and sent envoys, including his latest favourite Hugh Despenser, to negotiate a fresh truce with the Scots. Despenser, Pembroke and the Bishop of Ely met the Scottish delegates at Berwick and arranged a truce to last for two years. Edward undertook to destroy Harbottle Castle, which the Scots considered a menace to their safety. Robert, in turn, undertook not to build any castles on the Scottish side of the border—a meaningless gesture since he had no intention of doing so and his previous policy had always been to demolish castles whenever the Scots captured them. But this negative point was the only clause which Edward could secure and it was something of a face-saver. It must have been small consolation for Edward, faced with a further outbreak of trouble among his barons.

The truce was signed on 22nd December 1319 and a month later the Pope intervened, summoning Robert and the leaders of the Scottish clergy to his court at Avignon to answer for their misdeeds. The summons was addressed to the "Noble lord Robert Bruce, governing the kingdom of Scotland"—a slight improvement over the previous form of address but not enough for Robert to take the document seriously. The Pope retaliated by ordering the Bishops of London and Carlisle to excommunicate King Robert. The four leading Scottish prelates—the Bishops of St. Andrews, Dunkeld, Aberdeen and Moray—were likewise excommunicated on political .rather than religious grounds. The actual excommunications were not pronounced until 16th June 1320, almost six years to the day after Bannockburn, but in the previous months the Scots countered the papal tirades with an impressive show of national solidarity, a political landmark as important as Bannockburn had been a military one.

Chapter XIII

Arbroath and After

Five years after the murder of Thomas à Becket, King William the Lion founded an abbey in his memory, on the bank of the Brothock Water near its junction with the North Sea. Almost a century and a half later Arbroath Abbey was the venue for the drafting and signing of a document which has come to be regarded as Scotland's Declaration of Independence. Very little is known about the circumstances of the drafting of the document. Bower's chronicle mentions that the magnates of Scotland came together in a great assembly at the abbey, but he may just have assumed this since the letter was dated at Arbroath. The abbot of Arbroath was Bernard of Linton, Robert's chancellor, and many important state documents were dated from Arbroath in this period, indicating that the chancellery functioned there. It seems probable that Bernard drafted the letter, sent copies of it to the earls, barons and prelates for their signatures and seals. At least two copies of the document were prepared, one of which was despatched, on 6th April 1320, in the care of Sir Adam Gordon and Sir Edward de Maubuisson to the papal court at Avignon.

In appearance and content the Declaration of Arbroath was a masterpiece, a model statement of the right of a nation to govern itself as a free country. The document itself is impressive, in beautiful handwriting, with an array of beribboned seals in red and green wax. The style of the Latin is superb, lyrical without being effusive, concise but stately. In the name of eight earls (Caithness, Fife, Lennox, March, Moray, Ross, Strathearn and Sutherland), thirty-one barons and the whole community of the realm of Scotland, the letter recounted the history of Scotland since the earliest times—how the Scots had come from Scythia, via Spain to the outermost limits of Europe; how they had been converted to Christianity by Saint Andrew himself and therefore had a special relationship with the papacy. In the most courteous terms they reminded the pope of this and also of his responsibility, as Father of Christendom and God's Vicegerent, to do equal justice to all nations. The document was sent in the names of the Second and Third Estates of Scotland; the clergy were conspicuous by their absence—but this may be explained by the fact that the bishops had their own fight with the papacy at that time and as that matter was *sub judice* they deemed it prudent to steer clear of a temporal matter, the Pope's interference in the quarrel between Scotland and England.

After recounting the horrors and hardships suffered under English rule, the letter concludes in ringing tones:

> At length it pleased God, who alone can heal after wounds, to restore us to liberty from these innumerable calamities, by our most serene prince, king and lord, Robert, who for the delivering of his people and his own rightful inheritance from the enemies' hand, did, like another Joshua or Judas Maccabeus, most cheerfully undergo all manner of toil, fatigue, hardship and hazard. The divine providence, the right of succession by the laws and customs of the kingdom (which we will defend till death), and the due and lawful consent and assent of all the people, made him our king and prince. To him we are obliged and resolved to adhere in all things, both on account of his right and his own merit, as being the person who hath restored the people's safety in defence of their liberties. But, after all, if this prince shall leave these principles he hath so nobly pursued, and consent that we of our kingdom be subjected to the king or people of England, we will immediately endeavour to expel him as our enemy, and as the subverter both of his own and our rights, and will make another king who will defend our liberties. For so long as there shall but one hundred of us remain alive, we will never consent to subject ourselves to the dominion of the English. For it is not glory, it is not riches, neither is it honour, but it is liberty alone that we fight and contend for, which no honest man will lose but with his life.

The determination expressed in this document shows the community of the realm speaking with one voice and, in the light of subsequent events, there was unconscious irony in the threat to make another man king if Robert deserted the principles he had so nobly pursued. The signatories of the Declaration included men, like Douglas, Moray, Hay, Keith and Walter Stewart who had been Robert's closest comrades in arms; but many of the other names, surprisingly, were of men whose loyalty to the king was far less certain and even men like Ingelram de Umfraville who had long been bitter opponents of Robert. Many staunch supporters of the king were not among the signatories of the Declaration and, conversely, a high proportion of those who did sign were involved in a conspiracy against the king within a matter of months.

The causes of this disaffection are obscure, but it is probable that Edward II, having failed to subjugate Scotland by force of arms, tried to emulate his father by placing a puppet ruler on the throne—one who would be more amenable to his demands. The candidate for this doubtful honour was Sir William de Soules, the hereditary Butler and great-nephew of the Guardian Sir John de Soules. William was the son of Nicholas de Soules, one of the unconsidered claimants of 1291–2, the claim being based on the questionable legitimacy of his grandmother Marjorie, half-sister of Alexander III. The conspiracy involving members of the old Balliol-Comyn faction, was doomed to failure from the outset. Even if they had managed to oust King Robert the people of Scotland would have rallied to him far more enthusiastically now than they did in 1306 when he seized the throne. Anyone usurping the throne by murdering the king would soon have found his position untenable.

Murdoch Menteith, brother of Earl Alan of Menteith and a Scot who had chosen to remain at the English court, got wind of the plot and immediately rode north. His motive for risking his life to return to Scotland and visit Robert is not known, but disgust at the thought of a dastardly conspiracy is unlikely to have been the reason. His brother was dead and the earldom had devolved on his daughter Mary. Significantly Murdoch received the forfeited lands of the principal conspirators after the plot was exposed, and in 1323 his niece resigned the earldom to him.

Apart from de Soules himself the principal plotters included the Countess of Strathearn. According to Barbour the plot was revealed by an unspecified lady, but Fordoun names her as

Lady Strathearn; perhaps she committed some minor indiscretion which gave the game away. Her husband, though not directly involved in this plot, had been a Commissioner for Balliol in the Great Cause, had sided with Edward I during the Comyn wars, joined Robert soon after his coronation but defected to the English again after the battle of Methven. Another conspirator was David de Brechin, a nephew of Comyn of Buchan. Known as the Flower of Chivalry, he had fought alongside Robert Bruce in the attack on Lochmaben Castle in 1299, but after Robert seized the throne he joined the Balliol faction in the English camp until 1312. According to Barbour, Sir David was not one of the conspirators, but had heard mention of the plot and committed the sin of not passing on the information to the king. The other plotters consisted of Gilbert Malherbe, John Logie, Richard Broun and Roger de Moubray.

News of the conspiracy roused general condemnation. The so-called Black Parliament was called at Scone on 4th August and the conspirators tried and sentenced. Five men arraigned before the judges were subsequently acquitted; they included Patrick Graham and Eustace Maxwell, two of the signatories of the Declaration of Arbroath. De Soules and the Countess of Strathearn were condemned to imprisonment for life. Malherbe, Logie, Broun and Brechin were found guilty of treason and were subsequently drawn on hurdles to the place of execution, hanged and beheaded. Roger de Moubray died before he could be brought to trial, so his corpse was exhibited before the judges so that they could pronounce sentence and the forfeiture of his lands. The judges would have had the body hanged and beheaded, but King Robert intervened and allowed the corpse to be interred without further ceremony. The execution of Sir David Brechin upset Umfraville who denounced his fealty to Robert. Characteristically, the king allowed him time to see to his old friend's funeral and sell up his Scottish estates before departing, under safe conduct, to England. Edward II restored his English estates, maintaining the fiction that he had never really left his English allegiance.

The conspiracy left a nasty taste in the mouth. Four of the signatories of the Declaration had been found guilty of treason, another two had been suspected and a seventh had left the country in disgust. Nevertheless this sorry episode does not detract from the fact that the Declaration itself deserves to be regarded as one of the finest examples of a national testament ever produced. The de Soules affair, however, was the death-throes of the long-standing feud between the Bruce and Balliol-Comyn factions—at least in the lifetime of King Robert.

The Arbroath Declaration had a profound effect on Pope John, though he was still not ready to give Robert his due recognition. The Pope replied at the end of August skilfully avoiding the thorny issue of Robert's status. At the same time, however, he wrote to Edward II and referred to Robert as "ruler of the kingdom of Scotland"—an improvement over previous phraseology but still short of the coveted "King of Scots" which Robert so desired. Encouraged by the Pope's evasive answer Robert sent envoys to Avignon, hoping for recognition and the removal of the ban of excommunication, but the Pope refused to grant them an audience. In September Edward made a tentative peace overture, sending a four-man commission headed by Archbishop Melton to Carlisle to discuss a lasting peace with the Scots. As usual the talks got bogged down on the question of suzerainty and the discussions ended without achieving anything.

Early in the new year Pope John recovered from his conciliatory mood of the previous August and began fulminating against the Scots once more, with more than usual gusto. In February he despatched no fewer than six bulls to Edward, directing that *all* invaders of England should be excommunicated, that the twice-accursed Robert Bruce be excommunicated once more, and that the Scottish prelates should be compelled to come before the papal court at Avignon. Edward used the threat of excommunication in a curious manner. He sent word to the Earl of Atholl (still supporting the English cause) and Andrew Harcla, telling them to receive into the king's peace those Scots who were bothered by the excommunication. Very few Scots took this spiritual bribe, among them being Alexander de Moubray, a relative of the de Soules conspirator.

Peace negotiations dragged on desultorily during 1321 but without result. Edward's position was irreparably weakened by his long-running dispute with his barons. In 1321 the dispute erupted into civil war. Humphrey de Bohun and the other

Marcher Earls took up arms against Edward and his favourites, the Despensers. The fighting, such as there was, was mainly confined to Wales. Towards the end of the year The Earl of Lancaster began preparing for an uprising, aimed at the deposition of the king. Shrewdly Earl Thomas sought Scottish support for his venture, in exchange for the recognition which Edward had denied the Scots and a permanent peace settlement. King Robert probably realized that little would come of this agreement, and said that he could never trust a man who had broken faith with his own lord, but anything which embarrassed Edward was worth trying, so he permitted Douglas and the Earl of Moray to negotiate with Lancaster, whom they quaintly addressed, in correspondence, as " King Arthur ". Details of a secret treaty between Scotland and the English barons were found in a document on the body of the Earl of Hereford who was slain in March 1322. Whether the Scots would have aided the rebellion is a matter for conjecture. Certainly, in January 1322, as soon as the two-years' truce had expired, Douglas and Moray led their hobelars across the Border and ravaged the northern counties. Although Lancaster had mustered a sizeable army in southern Yorkshire and could have dealt with the Scottish menace he turned his back on it. Edward, with uncharacteristic resoluteness, assembled an army, marched north and forced the rebel earls to retreat from Burton on Trent. The rebels retreated northwards, meaning to link up with the Scots, but Andrew Harcla, scraped together a force in Cumberland, slipped past the Scots and intercepted the rebels at Boroughbridge. The Earl of Hereford was killed and the Earl of Lancaster was captured, to be executed a week later. The victory at Boroughbridge, which has been described as a minor Bannockburn in its tactical execution, put fresh heart into Edward.

Now that he had defeated the opposition within his own country he was in no mood for prolonging the truce with the Scots. He wrote exuberantly to the Pope stating that he was now resolved to settle the Scots for once and for all, and was planning a large-scale invasion. He ordered a general mobilization of the feudal host for 24th July at Newcastle. Shortly before the appointed date the Scots impudently invaded England. Though they were repulsed at Carlisle by its earl (the redoubtable Harcla recently elevated to the peerage) they raided the north-west as far as Preston, before returning with a considerable quantity of loot, recrossing the Sark the day before the Newcastle rendezvous. This raid was led by King Robert in person, proof that when it came to lightning campaigns he could still teach his lieutenants a thing or two. Bruce's Cumbrian *blitzkrieg* lasted four weeks, but inflicted more damage than Edward during any of his major campaigns.

Robert, unlike Edward, learned from experience. When the English army crossed the Tweed at the beginning of August their progress to Edinburgh was unimpeded; but to their dismay the English soon found that the drastic Scottish policy of 'scorched earth' meant that there was nothing left for them to forage. Robert had organized the systematic evacuation of the countryside: all cattle had been driven off to a place of safety and what they could not remove the Scots burned, so as to deny any comfort to the enemy. The English themselves sacked the Abbey of Holyrood on the outskirts of Edinburgh, but that was small consolation. According to Barbour the English captured only one lame cow, browsing peacefully in a field near Tranent, and this led the Earl of Surrey to remark that this was the dearest beef he had ever seen: "Surely it has cost a thousand pounds and more!" The main Scottish army withdrew north of the Forth, but raiding parties continually harried the English lines of communications. Famine broke out among the English ranks and Edward was forced to admit defeat without having engaged the Scottish forces. In September the English army began its long retreat. An attempt to bring supplies in by sea was defeated by contrary winds. On the way south the English made half-hearted attempts to sack the abbeys of Melrose and Dryburgh, but Douglas and his commandos disturbed them in their sacrilegious activities and beat them off, inflicting heavy losses.

While the English army retreated down the east coast, Robert launched a major invasion of Cumberland on 1st October. As soon as the Scots set foot on the English bank of the Sark thousands of refugees as far south as the North Riding took to the roads in headlong flight—such was the terror which a Scots raid now inspired in them. Robert's army marched up the Eden valley from Carlisle and swept down into north Yorkshire, laying siege to Norham and Bamborough castles, ravaging County Durham and penetrating districts of Yorkshire where no Scots raiders had even been before. Learning of the whereabouts of the main English force, Robert regrouped his army at Northallerton on 12th October and advanced on Rievaulx Abbey, Edward's field headquarters. Edward sent out his army, under the command of the Earl of Richmond, John of Brittany, to check the Scottish advance. Robert found the English army drawn up on 14th October, on a steep, boulder-strewn hillside at Byland on the western side of Scawton Moor. Robert was faced with a dilemma. To make a detour to avoid this formidable obstacle would mean delay and Edward would escape. On the other hand a frontal attack up a steep slope against strong, entrenched positions, would be little short of suicidal. Robert chose the latter and sent Douglas and Moray with their men to charge up the slope. The ridge was defended by infantry under Sir Ralph Cobham, reckoned the best knight in England, and Sir Thomas Uhtred. Cobham was captured in the ensuing fighting, but the Englishmen hurled rocks down upon the attacking Scots and their archers posed a serious threat. Robert then sent in his nimble highlanders, to scale the crags and take the enemy in the rear higher up the slope—as they had done at the Pass of Brander. When they had scaled the heights and reached the level ground the highlanders found John of Brittany bringing up strong reinforcements. Without pausing to catch their breath the highlanders launched a wild charge. The English knights, taken completely by surprise, "fled like hares before greyhounds", as Grey sardonically described it, and Douglas and Moray pressed forward their assault. Cobham's men were now virtually surrounded, so they broke and fled. John of Brittany and many other English leaders were captured, but the big prize, Edward himself, eluded the Scots. They hotly pursued him all the way back to the very gates of York and though they did not capture him they inflicted a crushing humiliation which did not help his already tarnished image. Again the English baggage trains fell into Scottish hands, amply compensating the Scots for any damage they had suffered as a result of Edward's recent campaign in Lothian. The Scots returned to Scotland in leisurely fashion, pillaging the countryside systematically as was their custom and holding Beverley to blackmail before recrossing the Border on 2nd November.

Robert's treatment of his prisoners is interesting. John of Brittany had apparently spoken most disparagingly of the king and Robert, for his part, would have challenged him to single combat if he were not such a knave beneath his dignity. The hapless Earl of Richmond was kept prisoner for two years, and only released on payment of £20,000 ransom. At the battle of Byland the Scots had taken a number of prominent French lords and these men, by contrast, were hospitably treated by Robert and repatriated without ransom. This was a shrewd move, designed to drive a wedge between Edward and his French allies, and it paid off handsomely. The leading French prisoner, Henry de Sully, subsequently acted as intermediary in the resumed truce talks which led in the end to a semi-permanent settlement in May 1323. Despite Robert's reasonableness and de Sully's diplomacy Edward continued to act in his usual pigheaded fashion, aiming a studied insult at the Scottish king by addressing his correspondence to the people of Scotland and ignoring Robert altogether. A letter from Robert to de Sully regarding Edward's behaviour has been preserved and sheds illumination on the character of the Scottish leader—his unruffled good humour and his moderate yet resolute approach to the bloodymindedness of the Plantagenet:

> Robert, by God's grace king of Scotland, to the most noble Henry, lord of Sully, knight, his good friend, affectionate and loving greeting. You will recall, my lord, how it was stated in our letters sent to the king of England, and how also we informed you by word of mouth, that we desired and still desire at all times to negotiate with the king of England on a final peace between him and us, saving always to us and to our heirs our realm free and independent, and also the integrity of our allies. If the English king had been agreeable, we were willing to make a truce until Trinity [22nd May]. Regarding this, my lord, we have received your letters and transcripts of letters from the king of England declaring that he has "granted a truce to the people of Scotland who are at war with him". To us this is a very strange way of speaking. In earlier truces, even though the English king has not deigned to call us king, we have at least been named as the principal on one side, as he has on the other. But it does not seem advisable to us to accept a truce in which no more mention is made of us than the humblest man in our kingdom, so that we could demand no more than any other if the truce were to be infringed wholly or in part.

Robert was in a much stronger position than Edward and could afford to dictate terms. But Edward continued to display that petulance and truculence which bedevilled Anglo-Scottish relations so long as he lived. Lesser men, closer to the situation than Edward at Westminster, sought ways and means of resolving the problem. Apart from the intrigues of Lancaster, which were blatantly in his own interest, the first definite proposals for a settlement based on recognition of King Robert came from a surprising quarter. Andrew Harcla, Earl of Carlisle and Warden of the Western March, could not be accused of cowardice, being one of the few English leaders with the ability to stand up to the Scots. But he had sense enough to realize that continual Scottish depradations of northern England would result in the economic ruin of that region and recognition of Robert's kingship seemed a small price to pay for a solution to the problem. Accordingly Harcla crossed the Solway and met King Robert and the Earl of Moray at Lochmaben on 3rd January 1323. A treaty was drawn up stating that Scotland and England were to have their own kings, independent of each other. Harcla went much farther, however, and undertook to support Robert against all enemies. A commission of twelve men was to be appointed, six Scots and six Englishmen, to administer the peace settlement. If Edward assented to this agreement within a year, Robert was to pay the surprisingly generous sum of 40,000 marks as an indemnity and marry his heir-male (Queen Elizabeth was pregnant at last) to an English princess of Edward's choice. A copy of this agreement was subsequently sent to Edward, whether by Harcla or—more probably—by an enemy of Harcla's is not known. At any rate this document served as the principal exhibit at Harcla's trial for treason. In February Harcla was seized treacherously, tried and subjected to the usual judicial barbarity suffered by traitors. His quarters remained on grisly public exhibition for the inordinately long time of five years before his sister was permitted to have the remains for burial. Harcla had acted treasonably but in the best interests of his country and not for private gain. He had made no attempt to conceal his plans and his actions had a large measure of popular support. But he had dared to act on his own initiative, running counter to the will of his liege lord—and Edward took a horrible vengeance on him for his temerity.

Nevertheless the fact that the Harcla proposals had popular support was not lost on Edward or his advisers and reluctantly they were forced to agree to a truce on 30th May. The truce arranged at Bishopthorpe and ratified by Robert at Berwick a week later, was designed to run for thirteen years. Despite the length of the period envisaged the truce could be no more than a temporary device, to take the heat out of the situation. No attempt was made to concede the independence which the Scots had so decisively won. Edward was to remain obstinate to the last, no matter what defeats and humiliation the Scots inflicted on him. Abroad, Edward no longer enjoyed the whole-hearted sympathy of Pope John who was now negotiating with the Scots, and his relations with the French had become disrupted by the minor and obscure War of Saint Sardos which dragged on until 1325.

At the end of 1323 the Earl of Moray, accompanied by Henry de Sully, went to Avignon to resume negotiations with the Pope. The exact purpose of the visit, however, appeared to be quite different. Moray, in fact, sought from the Pope permission to go crusading in the Holy Land. John pointed out that as Moray, along with the other Scots, had been excommunicated this was out of the question, but suggested that if Moray made some attempt to secure a peace with England he would do his best for him. Moray replied that what his country wanted was peace with the Church. He then produced the proposal from King Robert, that he wished to mount a crusade himself, jointly with Charles IV, the new king of France. Again John replied that this was impossible until Robert had made his peace with the Church. Moray pointed out that this was exactly what King Robert wanted—but that the clerical error in the address of papal bulls to the Scots meant that they had gone astray. If the Holy Father would see to it that the letters were henceforward properly addressed, Moray would undertake that the king would receive them. Thus cornered the Pope had no alternative but to give way. With this promise of a new crusade Robert got recognition from the Pope, and this effectively undermined the continuing opposition of Edward. The Pope wrote to Edward explaining that recognition of the King of Scots in no way undermined Edward's position, but Edward was in no way mollified by this letter. On All Fools Day 1324 Edward wrote to the Pope, bleating about the scandalous conduct of the Holy See and whining that Scotland had belonged to him for a damned long time. Although the Pope refused to accede to Edward's impudent demand that no one should be appointed to a bishopric in Scotland without his permission, he allowed the interdict to remain in force until 1328. But recognition, even at the expense of excommunication, was a considerable diplomatic victory for the Scots—and Edward knew it.

Robert's queen had by now borne him two daughters, Maude and Margaret, but the son for which he and the country yearned had been denied him. Robert had not remained celibate during the eight years of the queen's imprisonment, and as a result of his liaisons in that period he had at least two natural sons, Neil of Carrick and Sir Robert Bruce. But then, on 5th March 1324, Queen Elizabeth gave birth to a boy, and the king and country rejoiced. The baby was christened David in memory of his illustrious ancestors, King David I and the Earl of Huntingdon. The birth of a son seemed to herald a new era, of settled government and—perhaps—lasting peace.

CHAPTER XIV

Peace in Sight

HAVING STEADFASTLY refused to recognize Scotland as a separate entity, Edward took the curious step, in July 1324, of summoning Edward Balliol from his ancestral estates at Bailleul in Picardy. Nine years later Edward Balliol was to head a puppet régime in Scotland lasting almost five years, kept in power by the English troops of Edward III. In 1324, however, it seemed as though Edward II would stop at nothing to deny Robert the recognition which was his by rights. That he would even jeopardize his own claim to be king of Scotland, in pursuance of this vendetta against Robert is shown by the decision to bring Balliol over from France. For the moment Edward Balliol was allowed to live quietly in England and nothing more positive was done to advance his claim to the Scottish throne. Nevertheless, this rash act on Edward's part can scarcely have been designed to improve relations between Scotland and England.

The majority of history books skip quickly over the years 1325 and 1326, unmarked as they were by any outstanding events. Too great an emphasis is always laid on battles, raids and other feats of arms throughout the reign of King Robert and years of comparative tranquillity tend to be glossed over by the chroniclers who are our chief source for contemporary or near-contemporary material. From the surviving documentary material, however, it is clear that in these years the task of reconstruction was carried out as resolutely as Robert had conducted the struggle against the English. Parliaments were called at Scone in 1325 and at Cambuskenneth in 1326. The latter is memorable from the fact that the community of the realm was well represented, in the form of burgesses from the leading towns. It has often been stated that the Cambuskenneth parliament was the first attended by the Third Estate, but representatives of the burghs were present at Balliol's *colloquium* of 1296 at which the treaty with France was drafted, and it is possible that burgesses attended one or more of the parliaments called from 1312 onwards, though the writs of summons have not been preserved.

The settled nature of the country was proved by Robert's decision, some time in 1325, to build himself a palace, at Cardross near Dumbarton. For the first twenty years of his reign Robert had led something of a nomadic existence, living rough with his troops in the field or flitting from one fortress or castle to the next. Now that the likelihood of English invasion seemed remote he could relax and permit himself some of the comforts normally enjoyed by a man of his rank. His palace at Cardross had windows of glass—an unheard of luxury in fourteenth-century Scotland—fine tapestries and decorated panelling. Here Robert and his family could get away from affairs of state and enjoy hunting or boating in the Firth of Clyde. It was probably here that Elizabeth gave birth to her second son, inexplicably christened John, but unhappily he did not survive the critical period of infancy. In April 1326 the royal family suffered its second bereavement in a matter of months. Walter Stewart, husband of the late Princess Marjorie and one of Robert's most promising young men, died suddenly at Bathgate.

Another sign of the times was the restoration of existing castles and the building of new ones. Up to 1326 Robert was almost obsessed with the fear that such strongholds, in English hands, could be used for the subjugation of the country. Now that the Scots were in the ascendant the possibility of the English establishing garrisons all over Scotland seemed unlikely. One of the first of the new royal castles was erected on the hill above Tarbert in Argyll. Eleven years earlier Robert had sat in a ship dragged over the narrow isthmus on which Tarbert now stands, between Loch Fyne and the West Loch, repeating a feat of the Norse who claimed all land betwixt which and the mainland a ship might pass. In this manner they had successfully claimed the valuable peninsula of Kintyre.

Apart from regularizing the raising of revenue through taxation, the Cambuskenneth parliament passed a new act for the succession to the throne. Robert's son David, now two years old, was presented to his people and designated as successor to his father in place of young Robert Stewart, Marjorie's son. The history of Scotland might have been vastly different if Robert had not been passed over in favour of his baby uncle. The law of primogeniture was not, as yet, clearly established and in the circumstances the long minority of David II, with its attendant misfortunes, could have been avoided. King Robert and the magnates, prelates and community of the realm, however, could not have known what the future held in store for Scotland when this fateful decision was taken.

On the diplomatic front 1326 witnessed a renewal of the alliance with France. New men were coming to the fore as the king's civil servants and two of them were entrusted with the negotiations, along with the veteran diplomat, the Earl of Moray. Master Walter of Twynholm in Kirkcudbrightshire had succeeded Bernard of Linton as Chancellor and Master James Ben had succeeded Lamberton as Bishop of St. Andrews. The other envoy was Master Adam Murray who, two years later, became Bishop of Brechin. Their mission to the court of Charles IV resulted in the Treaty of Corbeil signed in April. By the terms of this alliance the Scots and the French bound themselves to give each other support in the event of war against England. Charles IV, with the Saint Sardos campaign fresh in his mind, was an anxious to secure the help of the Scots as they were to get his.

Meanwhile the dissolute reign of Edward II was rapidly reaching its climax. Edward had Hugh le Despenser and his French queen Isabelle had her lover, Roger Mortimer, with the custody of Prince Edward of Windsor. At the end of 1326 civil war broke out afresh. In September Isabelle and Mortimer landed in Essex from France, declaring that they had come to avenge the murder of Thomas of Lancaster and to expel the Despensers. Edward's followers deserted him and on 2nd October he fled from London to the west country where he took refuge in the younger Despenser's estates in Glamorgan. Isabelle and Mortimer pursued him relentlessly and captured the Despensers whom they hanged from the highest gallows available. Edward made a futile attempt to escape by sea but was captured on 16th November and subsequently confined in Kenilworth Castle. Isabelle summoned a parliament to Westminster on 20th January. To keep everything nice and legal the captive king was compelled to abdicate in favour of his fourteen-year-old son. The government of Isabelle and Mortimer, in the name of Edward III, was so weakly established, however, that they dared not leave the deposed king alive. On 3rd April he was taken from Kenilworth and handed over to two henchmen of Mortimer. Eventually he was incarcerated in Berkeley Castle in Gloucestershire. Every indignity was inflicted on him and he was systematically ill-treated and starved in the hope that he would die of disease. When his robust constitution seemed likely to prevail over this regimen he was cruelly put to death on 21st September. A red-hot poker was thrust *per anum* into his bowels so that the death wound would not be visible, but one can imagine the agonies which the wretched Edward must have suffered at the point of death.

With the abdication of Edward II the truce between him and Robert automatically lapsed. In order to remind the English that they still had the upper hand the Scots were not slow in resuming operations in northern England, choosing the very day of Edward III's coronation (1st February) for a dramatic attack on Norham Castle. The assault failed only because a Scot in the garrison learned of the impending attack and warned the constable. The Scottish attack was beaten off, but it was a salutary reminder to the English and it had the desired effect. On 15th February the newly appointed council of regency passed an act for the prolongation of the truce on the English side of the Border and followed this with a unilateral declaration on 6th March affirming that the truce was still in force. Nevertheless, although the Scots did not follow up the abortive assault on Norham, Robert did not regard the truce as still binding and he took steps for the resumption of the raids into England in the summer of 1327, notwithstanding the fact that he was by now a very sick man.

The reason for the new policy of aggression on Robert's part was the persistent activities of English pirates in the North Sea. Cases of attack on Scottish shipping were becoming increasingly frequent and the trade, which was blossoming between Scotland and the countries of northern Europe, was in danger of being seriously impaired unless some decisive action were taken. As soon as the campaigning season was opened Robert began massing his troops along the Border in preparation for an all-out attack on northern England. The timing of the Scottish offensive has been queried by some historians, and the theory has been advanced that Robert was now so ill that his moderate policies were overruled by the 'hawks', Douglas and Moray. The facts, however, belie this, for Robert was certainly well enough to make a trip to Ulster in July of that year and force the Anglo-Irish seneschal, Sir Henry Mandeville, to make a truce with the Scots for one year and to undertake to supply them with agricultural produce.

The regents of England took steps to counter the Scottish menace and raised a formidable army which Froissart estimated at 30,000, including 8,000 heavy cavalry—though these figures seem exaggerated. Part of this force included 2,500 German and Flemish knights, under the command of John of Hainault, for which the English treasury had budgeted £14,000. The English also had the latest thing in siege engines—the 'crakkis of war' or cannon, the first occasion on which gunpowder was to be used in an Anglo-Scottish campaign. According to Barbour the Scots were intrigued by the English artillery but were in no way deterred by it. The English force made its usual leisurely progress north. At York Queen Isabelle and her ladies threw a party for Hainault's Flemings—much to the disgust and rancour of the English rank and file who had no liking for foreigners and showed it. Fighting broke out between the two contingents and morale suffered accordingly.

On 15th June the Scots army crossed the Border, through the Kielder Forest of Northumberland and down the Tyne to Weardale. Robert himself did not take part in this campaign, but in addition to his veteran commanders there were Douglas's younger brother Sir Archibald and James Stewart, younger brother of the late Walter. The Scots ravaged the countryside as far as Appleby and then turned eastward again. The English army set out from York on 10th July and a week later were encamped at Durham where they could make out the smoke from the Scottish camp-fires. The regents tried to emulate the

Scots mobility by despatching squadrons of light cavalry, with the minimum of supplies, in search of their elusive enemy. For two days the English scouts combed the countryside in the vicinity of Blanchland without making contact with the Scots. Baffled by this the English commanders then decided to strike north and block the crossing of the Tyne to prevent the Scots from withdrawing. The main English force settled down at Haydon Bridge on 20th July to ambush the Scots, but a week passed without sight or sound of the Scots. During that period the weather was unduly inclement and the English morale sank even farther as the wretched soliders bivouacked in the marshy ground.

On 31st July an English esquire named Thomas Rokeby was on patrol a few miles from Allendale when he came upon the Scottish army. He was captured but promptly released and told to go ahead and let the English know where the Scots were waiting for them. That night the English army moved to Blanchland and the following day marched to the River Wear, on the southern bank of which the Scots were strongly entrenched. The Scots were deployed on two rounded promontories at the foot of which the Wear, now in spate, ran strongly. Edward III sent a herald to the Scots, asking them to come down and cross the river where he could do battle with them like men and promising that the English would not attack until they were safely across. The Scots declined this polite proposal. To do as Edward suggested might seem more manly but all was fair in love and war. Edward had a much bigger army and the Scots would be foolish to abandon such a fine position in those circumstances. Deadlock ensued for two days, though there was some lively skirmishing which went in the Scots' favour. On 3rd August, however, the English ambushed a large force in the woods behind the Earl of Moray. Douglas, realizing that they were in danger of being encircled, carefully carried out a withdrawal under cover of darkness. The campfires were stoked up so that the English would be unaware of the Scottish intentions. Then the army slipped silently away into the night and took up another and much stronger position about two miles away in Stanhope Park, a hunting preserve of the Bishop of Durham. The following night Douglas and a party of knights carried out a daring raid on the headquarters of Edward III and would have captured the boy-king had not the alarm been raised and the household bodyguard put up a stiff resistance. The following night the English army was on the alert, fearing another night attack in greater strength than before. There seemed to be a great deal of coming and going in the Scottish lines, with fires burning brightly and bugles calling out at frequent intervals. But in the cold grey light of the dawn the English saw that the Scots had mysteriously disappeared. Edward was so baffled and enraged at this unchivalrous conduct that he burst into tears. The Scots had got clean away, with enormous quantities of booty, and all the English had to show for the campaign were several hundred dead and wounded—not to mention the agues, rheumatism and colds sustained by their sojourn in the marshes. Edward had no alternative but to get his army back to York, disperse his levies and foot the bill for the expensive Continental mercenaries.

When the Scots returned to their base about the middle of August Robert had likewise returned from Ulster. On hearing their news he decided to press home his advantage and mounted a second campaign against the northern shires. He laid siege to Norham while his chief lieutenants besieged Alnwick and Warkworth. Though they failed to secure these objectives the Scots then proceeded to a pretty thorough harvest of northern England. Northumberland was completely devastated, while districts farther south were lucky to get off on payment of a stiff ransom which secured them respite until Whitsun 1328. It now seemed highly probable that Robert would not leave things at that, but intended nothing less than the complete annexation of Northumberland. Though no direct act of annexation ever took place it is clear that Robert made grants of land in Northumberland to several of his supporters.

Robert was still engaged in the siege of Norham Castle when, in mid-October, two English envoys came to him on behalf of the English court. Henry Percy of Alnwick and a lawyer named William of Denum were empowered by the council of regency to open talks aimed at a lasting peace. On 18th October Robert wrote to Edward III, setting out six points which would form the basis of a treaty:

1. King Edward and his barons must recognize that Robert I and his heirs for all eternity should have the kingdom of

Scotland " free, quit and entire ", without rendering homage.

2. Robert's son David to marry Edward's sister, Joan of the Tower.

3. No one in Scotland or England to hold lands in the other country.

4. A mutual pact to give military support to each other against all enemies (saving only Robert's existing commitments to France under the Treaty of Corbeil).

5. Robert to pay an indemnity of £20,000 within three years of peace being made.

6. The kings and councils of both countries to appeal to the Pope for the excommunication and interdict to be lifted from the Scots.

Robert promised that, if Edward would agree to these six points, he would send envoys to Newcastle to carry out the detailed negotiations. On 30th October Edward, then at Nottingham, gave his assent to peace talks being opened on two of the six points—the indemnity of £20,000 and the marriage of David and Joan. It was far short of what Robert wished, but it was a start. In the midst of these political manoeuvres Robert suffered a great personal loss. On 26th October his consort, Queen Elizabeth, died at Cullen in Banffshire. The queen was in her middle forties, and we are not told of what she died; but undoubtedly the years of her confinement, the strain attendant on being first lady in a country at perpetual war, and a succession of pregnancies relatively late in life combined to take their toll of her constitution. Elizabeth's body was embalmed, her entrails and organs being removed for burial in Cullen's Lady Kirk, and her corpse brought to her sorrowing husband at Dunfermline. Here she was laid to rest, alongside the kings and queens of Scotland from the time of Malcolm Canmore onward.

Edward's reply to Robert regarding the six points betrayed that obstinacy which had characterized his father and, had the Scots been percipient, indicated that the future of an independent Scotland would be uncertain and stormy. Robert had made generous proposals, dictated from a real position of strength. Edward, on the other hand, replied in haughty terms which belied the weakness of his position and agreed to two only of the points, reserving judgment on the vital question of recognition until the problems of disinheriting English nobles with Scottish estates and the projected military alliance were settled. The Scots terms were remarkably similar to those outlined in the so-called Harcla treaty of 1323—except, of course, that the proposed indemnity had dropped somewhat in value (from 40,000 marks or £27,000, to £20,000).

The English commissioners, headed by the Archbishop of York, were appointed on 23rd November, but the Scottish envoys did not receive their safe-conducts until 25th January 1328. After this delay, however, the talks proceeded briskly and the following month the Scottish delegates came to York where Edward was holding parliament. On 1st March Edward and his council drew up a preliminary document giving the recognition for which Robert had fought so dearly. After setting forth the terrible hardships inflicted on England and Scotland through the wars fought on this account Edward continued:

> We will and concede for us and all our heirs and successors, by the common counsel, assent and consent of the prelates, magnates, earls and barons and communities of our realm in our parliament that the kingdom of Scotland shall remain for ever separate in all respects from the kingdom of England, in its entirety, free and in peace, without any kind of subjection, servitude, claim or demand, with its rightful boundaries as they were held and preserved in the times of Alexander of good memory king of Scotland last deceased, to the magnificent prince, the lord Robert, by God's grace illustrious king of Scots, our ally and very dear friend, and to his heirs and successors.

Edward went on to renounce any rights which he had claimed in Scotland, cancelling any agreements regarding the subjection of Scotland and declaring null and void any documents relating to such agreements. At long last the king of England had proclaimed in no uncertain terms that Scotland was free—and by acknowledging Robert's right to the throne also implied that the elevation of John Balliol in 1292 had been wrong. John had owed his throne to a judgment of his paramount lord; Robert owed his throne to his own generalship. Thus there was no implication that somehow Robert owed his position to the king of England. The old concept of suzerainty over Scotland was thus laid to rest.

The treaty itself followed a fortnight later. Edward's commissioners had to travel north, to Edinburgh, for the final round of talks and the signing of the treaty. The commissioners, consisting of the Bishops of Lincoln and Norwich, Henry Percy, Sir Geoffrey le Scrope (Chief Justice of King's Bench) and William de la Zouche, reached the Scottish capital on 10th March with full powers to conclude and proclaim a final peace. Robert was ill again and confined to his bed in the monastery of Holyrood, and it was there, in the king's bedchamber, that the discussions were concluded on 17th March. The scene on that auspicious occasion must have been dramatic. Robert himself, now in the advanced stages of an incurable illness, nevertheless dominated the gathering. Grouped about him were six earls, the leading bishops, the principal officers of the royal household, and many of the barons and knights who had fought long and hard to see this moment of triumph.

The treaty was drawn up in Latin and French, and attached to it were two notarial documents regarding the £20,000 indemnity and Robert's letters-patent concerning the royal marriage settlement. In essence the terms of the Treaty of Edinburgh followed the six points outlined the previous winter, with the exception of the clause concerning the holding of lands in both Scotland and England. Although he personally stood to lose most by a ruling against the reinstatement of those who had lost estates as a result of the war, Robert had shown great statesmanship in this proposal, and it is to Edward's discredit that he allowed himself to be swayed on this point by certain English noblemen, such as Henry Percy and Henry Beaumont, who claimed lands in Scotland which had been forfeited during the war.

An interesting clause of the treaty showed the anxiety of the English to secure good relations with Scotland through the proposed royal marriage. If the marriage had not taken place by Michaelmas 1338 Robert undertook to pay an indemnity of £100,000—an impossible sum. The significance of the date is that David would by that time have passed his fourteenth birthday—the age of consent in those days. The Scots, however, had no desire to renegue on this part of the deal, any more than did the English, and arrangements were speedily put in hand for the royal wedding. The queen-dowager Isabelle and Princess Joan journeyed north in July 1328 and at Berwick on the 12th, the day following Robert's fifty-fourth birthday, the two young children were formally married in the presence of a great assembly of magnates from both countries. The bride was six-years old, her groom just four. As a magnanimous gesture (or an inducement to the Scots to let Beaumont and Percy have back their Scottish estates) Queen Isabelle promised to return the Stone of Destiny to Scotland, but the London mob forcibly prevented its removal from Westminster Abbey and the matter was subsequently dropped. The stone lay under the Coronation Chair until 1951, when Scottish nationalists removed the red sandstone block and spirited it back to Scotland. It was later recovered from Arbroath Abbey, venue of the Declaration of Independence, and returned to London. At least the prophecy that Scottish sovereigns would continue to be crowned on it came true, when the Stewart king James VI became James I of England in 1603.

The Treaty of Edinburgh was ratified by the English parliament at Northampton on 4th May. Considering the bitterness and savagery of the preceding thirty years it was a remarkably fair settlement and had both parties adhered to it the history of Britain might have been much less sanguinary in the ensuing centuries. As it was, the dispute over the forfeited estates of Percy and Beaumont escalated into war four years later and Edward unilaterally broke the treaty, taking the advantage of his brother-in-law's minority to set up a puppet régime under Edward Balliol. The events of 1333–8 set at naught all the efforts of the preceding generation and almost a century was to pass before the Scots and English could agree to another peace treaty. Even then the peace was of short duration and the hatred which had been engendered in the period fom 1296 to 1328 was to erupt time and time again for hundreds of years.

The Scots had won their independence, but at a terrible cost in manpower and resources. In the 42 years since the death of Alexander III the commercial, economic and cultural development of Scotland had stagnated or been reversed. To be sure the resilience of the Scots had enabled them to make a remarkable recovery after Bannockburn and the settled government and efficient administration of the country from then onwards testify to the statesmanship of King Robert. In terms of casualties the English lost more men in the actual fighting and in the subsequent Scottish raids; but if we accept a ratio of four to one for the respective populations then Scotland's loss was proportionately greater. Scots raids from 1314 to 1323 devastated the north of England as far south as the Humber; English penetration of Scotland at its greatest extent was as far north as Inverness—roughly the same degree of penetration on both sides. But the greater part of England, and the area of greatest wealth, population and development, lay well to the south of the Humber, whereas the greater part of Scotland was well within the area devastated periodically by English invasion.

In cold print dates mean little, but the Scottish struggle for independence and the English campaign for domination lasted 32 years. By contrast the French Revolutionary and Napoleonic Wars lasted 26 years. A modern analogy would be the struggle in Indo-china; Scotland was England's Vietnam. The war cost England more than can be assessed in concrete terms, but twelve major invasions and extensive garrisons over more than a generation must have caused a terrific drain on manpower and resources. The unsuccessful prosecution of the Scottish wars led to bitter dissension inside England, ending in civil war and the murder of a king. But more important than that was the loss of prestige suffered by England in the world at large. The Hundred Years War with France might never have happened but for the humiliation inflicted on England by the Scots; assuredly the French would never have won that struggle had it not been for the help, both military and diplomatic, which Scotland gave to its old ally. After three centuries of fighting all that England gained were the Isle of Man and the town of Berwick, now a mere shadow of its former maritime importance. On the debit side was a legacy of bitterness which time has never quite eradicated. Yet, had the peace of 1328 been given a chance to work, the hostility which bedevilled Anglo-Scottish relations would probably have died out within a generation.

It was Scotland's great good fortune to have found a leader such as Robert Bruce in her darkest hour; it was Scotland's great tragedy that her illustrious champion should be taken from her in his hour of triumph.

CHAPTER XV

The End of the Reign

FOR ROBERT time was running out. He was given only thirteen months in which to enjoy peace and recognition, and even as the Treaty of Edinburgh was being signed he knew that he had not long to go. He intended being present at his son's wedding, and ordered fine raiment and costly jewels for the occasion, but a recurrence of the " great malady " of which the chroniclers hint, prevented his attendance on that solemn occasion. In August, however, he rallied sufficiently to make yet another trip to Ireland, no mean undertaking for anyone in those times. We can only speculate about the purpose of his visit to Ulster. It cannot be denied that Ireland occupied an important place in his foreign policy and the ill-starred campaign of 1315–18 shows that the Scots were not above attempting to subordinate Ireland to themselves, much as the Plantagenets tried to subjugate Scotland. The campaign that ended so disastrously at Dundalk in 1318, however, may be seen as the expression of the reckless ambition of Edward Bruce and his elder brother was content latterly to secure the goodwill of the Irish and to appeal to the ancient ties of race and language, rather than bind Scotland and Ireland more closely in political terms.

Robert returned to Scotland before the winter and was in residence at Cardross for Christmas. The efforts of his journey were too much, and his ailment severely curtailed his activities, but the following February he made a partial recovery. He knew that he was dying, but he was determined to pay one last visit to that part of the country where he had been born and had spent his childhood. On 6th February he set out from Girvan, on the borders of Carrick and Galloway, for a pilgrimage to the shrine of Saint Ninian, the missionary who had brought Christianity to Scotland in the fifth century, long before the time of the Irish Columba. The ailing king was borne slowly and painfully on a litter to Inchmichael (near present-day Castle Kennedy in Wigtownshire). There he had a relapse and was forced to tarry for about a month. When he was well enough to be moved his faithful retainers carried him on, across Wigtownshire, arriving at Whithorn on 1st April where he spent four or five days, fasting and praying to Saint Ninian. Thence the royal entourage journeyed northwards, across Galloway—perhaps passing close to Glen Trool where he had first defeated the English 23 years earlier—and returned to Cardross at the end of April. In the five weeks that yet remained to him Robert methodically put his affairs in order. His little son, now Earl of Carrick like his father and grandfather before him, was given his own court at Turnberry and it was either here, or at Cardross, that the magnates of the realm came to do homage to the lad who would so soon succeed to the throne.

The king died on 7th June 1329, a few weeks short of his fifty-fifth birthday. A great deal of mystery surrounds the nature of Robert's illness. Contemporary writers speak merely of a great malady and it is not until the Lanercost Chronicle and Grey's Scalacronica, written a generation later, that leprosy is mentioned. That Robert was not, in fact, suffering from this hideous illness which filled the medieval mind with dread and loathing, is demonstrated—in a negative sense—by the fact that no attempt was made to segregate the king in the customary fashion. In the Middle Ages fear of leprosy was such that those unfortunate enough to contract it were treated like living dead: strictly segregated, regardless of rank or position, forced to wear special clothing and to carry a rattle to warn people of their approach, and forbidden to speak to anyone unless he were upwind of the person addressing him. These regulations were strictly enforced, yet no mention is made of them in relation to King Robert, and the fact that he was able to carry on affairs of state, make hazardous journeys and pilgrimages in the company of his courtiers, precludes leprosy as his disease. Even allowing for his exalted status and for the very great veneration in which his subjects held him, these factors would not have

M

conferred any immunity from the rigorous code to which lepers—even royal lepers like Baudouin of Jerusalem—were subjected. Besides, leprosy was a disease which took ten years on average to kill a man—yet the earliest reference to the king's illness occurs a bare two years before his death.

Barbour says that the king's illness "began through a benumbing brought on by his cold lying" during the period, from 1306 to 1309 when he was a fugitive in the heather. Agnes Mure Mackenzie clutches at this straw and deduces from it that Robert probably contracted pleurisy or pneumonia in the summer of 1328, and the hard winter of 1328–9 finished him off; but this ignores the fact that the king had suffered intermittently from 1327 onwards to such an extent that his conduct of the war was seriously impaired, and even pneumonia would not be described in the terms used by the chroniclers.

A recent examination of the skull of King Robert reveals pitting and extensive damage to the upper jaw and nose which indicate that Robert suffered considerable disfigurement in the last years of his life. In fact, in light of this evidence, it would appear that Robert's mysterious affliction was some form of syphilis. This possibility has previously been overlooked because it was thought that this venereal disease was not brought to Europe until the closing years of the fifteenth century, but due consideration is not always given to the manner in which disease changes its nature in the course of the centuries. The nature of the syphilitic epidemic which ravaged Europe in the 1490s was very different from the syphilis of the present day. There is now little doubt that syphilis was sporadic in Europe long before the great outbreak and the symptoms were probably more like those of the fifteenth century than today. By the same token leprosy is also a disease which has changed its appearance over the centuries. At this remove in time it is difficult to determine whether the 'unclean ailment' of the Middle Ages might not have been, in many instances, not leprosy but syphilis.

The possibility of the king having contracted a sexually transmitted disease cannot be ruled out. Philandering in that age and in those circumstances did not have the stigma which later became attached to it. Like other medieval rulers Robert openly acknowledged his bastard progeny, granting them lands and honours. Many of the great prelates of the medieval church were the natural sons of kings and princes; unable to inherit land on account of their illegitimacy they sought, and received, advancement in the church. For example Geoffrey Plantagenet, Archbishop of Canterbury, was the bastard son of Henry II. Barbour has a reference to Robert's dalliance with the ladies:

> And mony tyme, as I herd say
> Throw wemen that he wyth wald play . . .

It is therefore feasible that Robert contracted the primary form of syphilis during his nomadic existence and that the disease, in its secondary and tertiary forms, recurred at intervals throughout the rest of his life until it finally killed him.

The king's body was duly embalmed, but before this took place his heart was removed and placed in a silver box, for a special purpose. In the words of Froissart, as the king lay dying,

> He called to him the gentle knight Sir James Douglas, and said before all the lords, Sir James, my dear friend, ye know well that I have had much ado in my day to uphold and sustain the right of this realm, and when I had most ado I made a solemn vow, the which as yet I have not accomplished, whereat I am right sorry. The which was if I might achieve and make and end of all my wars, so that I might once have brought this realm in rest and peace, that I promised in my mind to have gone and warred on Christ's enemies, adversaries to our holy Christian faith . . . And sith it is so that my body cannot go nor achieve that my heart desireth, I will send the heart instead of the body to accomplish mine avow instead of myself; and because I know not in all my realm no knight more valiant than ye be, nor of body so well furnished to accomplish mine avow instead of myself, therefore I require you, mine own dear and special friend, that ye will take on you this voyage for the love of me . . .

National exigencies had baulked the finest knight in Christendom of his dearest wish, to take the cross and go to the Holy Land to fight the Saracens. The next best thing was to have his heart interred in the Holy Sepulchre in Jerusalem. While Douglas and his élite band of knights prepared for the long and hazardous journey the king's heartless body was borne in state across Scotland and laid to rest on 7th November, beside his wife, in Dunfermline Abbey. The corpse was buried under the middle of the choir and over it was erected a magnificent tomb which Robert had commissioned in Paris. And there Scotland's great king lay for over two centuries, until the zealots of the Reformation, in a fit of iconoclasm, destroyed the tombs of the Scottish kings and queens and severely damaged the structure of the abbey. The magnificent tomb was broken up and its material scattered to the four winds. Miraculously, however, the remains of King Robert buried below were left undisturbed. They lay there in the ruins of the abbey for a further 250 years. Then, in 1819, workmen repairing the floor of the abbey uncovered the skeleton of a man on the spot which tradition had assigned to Robert Bruce. The skeleton was exhumed and examined by an Edinburgh surgeon, Robert Liston. A portion of the breast-bone had been sawn away, in order to remove the heart, and this proved conclusively that the remains were indeed those of King Robert. From the measurement of the femur Liston estimated that Robert had been almost six feet tall and this anthropomorphic error has been perpetuated by many nineteenth-century writers. More recent calculations, however, show that Robert was about 5 feet 6 inches in height—and this tallies with his custom of riding a palfrey rather than a great destrier. People always like to think of their heroes as giants in the physical as well as metaphorical sense, and undoubtedly William Wallace came into this category; but Robert was of average stature for his times.

A cast of the skull was taken by W. Scoular, a pupil of the sculptor Chantrey, and this is now in the Anatomical Department of Edinburgh University. Rather inferior casts were made from this one, and are now in the Royal College of Surgeons, London and in Abbotsford House among the heterogeneous accumulation of relics gathered together by Sir Walter Scott, that magpie *par excellence*. Karl Pearson's study of the skull corroborates what we know of the character of King Robert. The mastoids were extremely massive and Pearson could not recall ever having seen a skull so well developed in the region of the union. The skull has great breadth and solidity, with a retreating forehead, suggesting a man of exceptional muscularity and strength, with a bull neck and ardent passions. Yet this massiveness was not purely animal in its nature. The development in the region of the obelion, lateral and posterior aspects show features which one associates with strong mental qualities.

The skull thus indicates great personal prowess and large organizational powers.

The workmen who stumbled on the coffin hastily covered it up again, pending a proper examination. When this took place soon afterwards a plaque was found on the lid, inscribed in Latin with the name of Robert King of Scots and this was naïvely accepted as confirmation. Subsequently it was realized that this was a hoax, but fifty years elapsed before the perpetrators of this prank confessed their guilt. At worst this jape only tended to sow seeds of doubt in the minds of scholars at the time, but the anatomical evidence of the missing sternum served to identify the skeleton positively. The faked coffin plate is still preserved in the National Museum of Antiquities, Edinburgh. The same museum has the stone head of a royal personage, recovered from the ruins of Dunfermline Abbey and this has been put forward tentatively as a contemporary likeness of Robert, probably from the Parisian tomb. But this is mere speculation, and the fact remains that of Scotland's greatest king there are no authentic portraits. The nearest approach would be the profile shown on his coinage. From the evidence of coin hoards it would appear that coins were not minted in Scotland till after the recovery of Berwick in the latter part of the reign. The portraiture on medieval coins, however, was crude and at best can give us no more than a caricature.

The earliest proper portraits of King Robert are probably those in two manuscripts, both of which show the king with his two wives. The Seton Armorial in Winton Castle, and the armorial in the National Library, Edinburgh, were drawn posthumously though the similarity of certain features indicates that they were based on the recollections of people who had known Robert in his lifetime. All subsequent portraiture, from the warlike painting in Taymouth Castle to the Bannockburn equestrian statue and the current Clydesdale Bank £1 note can only be described as artists' impressions, in which a greater or lesser degree of licence has been taken. Perhaps some day, as the science of physiognomy develops, it may be possible to reconstruct a true likeness of King Robert from his skull.

Robert's last wish was destined to remain unfulfilled. In the spring of 1330 Sir James Douglas and his knights boarded a ship at Montrose and sailed across the North Sea to Sluys in

Flanders. The party escorting the embalmed heart of the Bruce consisted of one knight banneret (Douglas himself), seven other knights and twenty-six esquires. Douglas and his men remained on board ship at Sluys for twelve days, waiting for news of anyone willing to join them on their little crusade. Douglas had letters of protection from Edward III no less, and also a letter of commendation addressed to Alfonso XI, King of Castile and Leon, who was then fighting against the Moors of Granada. Douglas decided to go to Spain, help Alfonso and then, with his support, continue to Jerusalem. The Scots sailed from Flanders to Valencia and from there they rode to the headquarters of Alfonso in Seville where the campaign was then in progress. Alfonso welcomed the Scottish contingent and put Douglas in command of the foreign knights serving under his banner. On 25th March the Moorish army clashed with the Christians at Tebas de Ardales.

The Moors seemed to be falling back at one point and Douglas, thinking that they were retreating, ordered his cavalry to charge, hoping that the main Spanish force would follow. But Alfonso knew the Moorish tactics of feigning withdrawal in order to draw their opponents into a trap and he held his troops back. Too late the good Sir James realized that his men were cut off from the main body, and soon they were completely surrounded by a much stronger force of Moorish cavalry. The Scots fought desperately to the last, performing great feats of valour, but they were overwhelmed and slaughtered to a man. The only survivor of the Scottish contingent was Sir William Keith of Galston, who had broken an arm in an earlier skirmish and was thus out of the fight on that occasion. After the battle he rode among the slain, retrieving the precious casket and also the corpse of Douglas which he had embalmed and taken back to Scotland. Douglas's body was later interred in St. Bride's Church in Douglas and Sir James's natural son, Archibald the Grim had a splendid alabaster sarcophagus erected over him. The casket containing King Robert's heart went not to Dunfermline but to Melrose Abbey, a Cistercian foundation of 1136 to which the late king had been especially attached. The casket was interred under the east window of the chancel, and there it remained until 1385 when the abbey was despoiled by English invaders. What became of this precious relic is a matter for conjecture. The silver casket was no doubt melted down and its contents thrown away by the robbers.

By the terms of the Tailzie of 1326 Thomas Randolph, Earl of Moray assumed the office of Guardian of Scotland during the minority of King David II. Within three years Moray, the last of the great captains of the struggle for independence, was dead —not on the field of battle but, like Robert himself, in his bed. He was stricken down by illness while preparing to meet the latest threat of invasion from England, the prelude to a new and bitter war. In later years, however, men would look back to the reign of Good King Robert, when the phoenix rose from the ashes, and Scotland as a nation was forged in a long and desperate struggle which has few parallels in recorded history.

Select Bibliography

(a) Separate Works

Anderson, A. O., *Early Sources of Scottish History* (Edinburgh, 1922)

——*Scottish Annals from English Chroniclers* (London, 1908)

Bain, J., *Calendar of Documents relating to Scotland* (Edinburgh, 1881–8)

Barbour, John, *The Bruce* (edited by W. M. Mackenzie, London, 1909)

Barron, E. M., *The Scottish War of Independence* (Inverness, 1934)

Barrow, G. W. S., *Robert Bruce* (London, 1965)

Bliss, W. H., *Calendar of Entries in the Papal Registers relating to Great Britain and Ireland: Papal Letters* (London, 1893—)

——*Calendar of Entries in the Papal Registers relating to Great Britain and Ireland: Petitions to the Pope* (London, 1896)

Christison, Gen. Sir P., *Bannockburn: the Story of the Battle* (Edinburgh, 1962)

Cooper, Lord, *The Register of Brieves* (Edinburgh, 1946)

Cumming-Bruce, M. E., *Family Records of the Bruces*

Dowden, J., *The Bishops of Scotland* (Glasgow, 1912)

Dunbar, A. H., *Scottish Kings: a Revised Chronology of Scottish History* (Edinburgh, 1906)

Duncan, A. A. M., *Regesta Regum Scottorum, Volume V*

Easson, D. E., *Medieval Religious Houses in Scotland* (London, 1957)

Hailes, Lord (Sir David Dalrymple), *Annals of Scotland from the Accession of Malcom III surnamed Canmore to the Restoration of James I* (Edinburgh, 1776–9)

Laing, H., *Descriptive Catalogue of Ancient Scottish Seals* (Edinburgh, 1866)

Luard, H. R., *Flores Historiarum* (London, 1890)

Mackenzie, A. M., *Robert Bruce, King of Scots* (London, 1934)

Macpherson, D., *Rotuli Scotiae* (1814–19)

Palgrave, F., *Documents and Records illustrating the History of Scotland* (London, 1837)
Paul, Sir J. Balfour, *The Scots Peerage* (Edinburgh, 1909–14)
Polain, L., *Les vrayes chroniques de Messire Jehan le Bel* (Brussels, 1863)
Powicke, Sir M., *The Thirteenth Century 1216–1307* (Oxford, 1953)
Raine, J., *History and Antiquities of North Durham* (London, 1852)
Rymer, T., *Foedera Conventiones Literae et Cuiuscunque Generis Acta Publica* (London, 1816–69)
Stevenson, J., *Documents Illustrative of the History of Scotland* (Edinburgh, 1870)
——*Illustrations of Scottish History from the Twelfth Century to the Sixteenth Century* (Edinburgh, 1834)
——*Documents Illustrative of Sir William Wallace his Life and Times* (Edinburgh, 1841)
Stevenson, J. H. and Wood, M., *Scottish Heraldic Seals* (Glasgow, 1940)
Stones, E. L. G., *Anglo-Scottish Relations, 1174–1328. Some selected documents* (Edinburgh, 1964)
——*The Great Cause* (London, 1973)
Stuart, J., *The Exchequer Rolls of Scotland* (Edinburgh, 1878–1908)
Stubbs, W., *Annales Londonienses* (Volume I) and *Gesta Edwardi de Carnarvon* (Volume II) of *Chronicles of the reigns of Edward I and Edward II* (London, 1882–3)
Theiner, A., *Vetera Monumenta Hibernorum et Scotorum Historian Illustrantia* (Rome, 1864)
Thomson, T., *Inquisitionum ad Capellum Domini Regis Retornatatarum* (1811–16)
Watt, D. E. R., *Fasti Ecclesiae Scoticanae Medii Aevi* (St Andrews, 1959)

(b) Chronicles
Bower *Johannis de Fordun Scotichronicon cum Supplementis et Continuatione Walteri Bower,* ed. W. Goodall (Edinburgh, 1759)
Fordoun *J. de Fordun Cronica Gentis Scotorum,* ed. W. F. Skene (Edinburgh, 1871–2)
Guisborough *The Chronicles of Walter of Guisborough,* previously edited as the chronicle of Walter of Hemingford or Hemingburgh, ed. for the Royal Historical Society, by Harry Rothwell (London, 1957)
Holyrood *The Chronicle of Holyrood* (Scottish Historical Society, Edinburgh, 1938)
Lanercost *Chronicon de Lanercost,* ed. Maitland Club, Edinburgh, 1839)

Man *The Chronicle of Man and the Sudreys,* ed. P. A. Muhcn and Rev. Dr Gross (Manx Society, Douglas, 1874)

Melrose *The Chronicle of Melrose,* ed. A. O. Anderson, M. O. Anderson and W. Croft Dickinson (London, 1936)

Picts-Scots *The Chronicles of the Picts: Chronicles of the Scots,* ed. W. F. Skene (Edinburgh, 1867)

Pluscarden *Liber Pluscardensis,* ed. F. H. J. Skene (Edinburgh, 1877–80)

Rishanger *Chronica Willelmi Rishanger,* ed. H. T. Riley (London, 1865)

Scalacronica *Scalacronica* by Sir Thomas Grey of Heton Knight (Maitland Club, Edinburgh, 1836)

Wyntoun *Andrew Wyntoun, Orygynale Cronykil of Scotland,* ed. D. Laing (Edinburgh, 1872–9)

Index

C

D